The
War
That
Business
Must
Win

Philip B. Osborne and the Editors of BUSINESS WEEK

# The
# War
# That
# Business
# Must
# Win

McGraw-Hill Book Company
New York     St. Louis     San Francisco
Dusseldorf     London     Mexico
Panama     Sydney     Toronto

THE WAR THAT BUSINESS MUST WIN

1234567890    VBVB    7543210

# Foreword

"We are approaching the limits of what government
alone can do. Our greatest need is to reach beyond
government to enlist the concerned and the
committed. To match the magnitude of our tasks, we
need the energies of our people—enlisted not only in
grand enterprises, but more importantly, in those
small, splendid efforts that make headlines in the
neighborhood newspaper instead of the national
journal."

PRESIDENT RICHARD M. NIXON,
*1969 Inaugural Address*

DURING THE PAST SEVERAL YEARS, the pages of *Business Week*
have carried many articles describing some of the extraordinary
achievements of industry in such crucial areas as housing, race
relations, and pollution control. Hundreds of other American
corporations, large and small, have also put their minds and energies to the task of improving the country's social and physical
environment, as well as its economic well-being. In recognition

of these efforts—many of which, as President Nixon noted, never make the national journal—*Business Week* has established the *Business Week* Awards for Business Citizenship. The recipients of the 1969 awards—the magazine's first—are the subject of this book.

There are five awards:

■ One award goes to a man or woman in business who has shown exceptional leadership in directing the resources of private enterprise toward the solution of national problems.

■ Two awards go to corporations for their efforts in "human resources": education, health, rehabilitation, employment, youth programs, and projects for bettering race relations.

■ Two additional awards go to corporations that have made important contributions toward improving the country's physical environment. This includes such fields as housing, transportation, pollution control, recreation, and new communities.

Heading up the awards committee for 1969 was John W. Gardner, chairman of the Urban Coalition, former Secretary of Health, Education, and Welfare, and a man of deep and sensitive concerns for the quality of American life. Serving on his committee were five distinguished leaders representing business, labor, government, and education: George P. Baker, dean of the Graduate School of Business Administration at Harvard University; Joseph A. Beirne, president of the Communications Workers of America; Richard Hatcher, mayor of Gary, Ind.; J. Irwin Miller, chairman of Cummins Engine Co., Inc.; and Rudolph A. Peterson, president of Bank of America.

The five award recipients which they picked will serve, we hope, as examples to others in industry. William H. Wendel (Chapter 2), president of Carborundum Co., is providing personal leadership for the revitalization of Niagara Falls, N. Y. Levi Strauss & Co. (Chapter 3) and Western Electric Co. (Chapter 4) are helping minority individuals get better jobs and open their own businesses. American Metal Climax, Inc. (Chapter 5) is trying to preserve the natural environment, and Rouse Co. (Chapter 6) is creating a whole new environment.

At the first awards presentation, held in Manhattan's Plaza Hotel Oct. 29, 1969, John Gardner neatly summed up the importance of such involvement. Drawing attention to today's social and environmental ills, Mr. Gardner noted that most citizens lay much of the blame for these ills on what they conceive to be the Establishment. And the people they conceive to be the proprietors of the Establishment are top business leaders. "Business leaders themselves have no such exaggerated view of their power," Mr. Gardner said. "They know all too well that their capacity to control the course of events is limited . . . . But there are, as we all know, areas in which business can demonstrate its capacity to act responsibly. And when businessmen approach these areas, it's of crucial importance that they understand the nature of the public dissatisfaction."

As one typical problem area, Mr. Gardner cited air and water pollution. "I have found," he said, "that businessmen tend to exonerate themselves by pointing to the great economic difficulty of pollution control, emphasizing the obstacles to action on their part, and in general behaving as though they were dealing with a reasonable and only mildly impatient friend, one who is always willing to listen to a well-phrased argument." But that is not what they are up against, as Mr. Gardner pointed out. "They are facing something intangible but potentially explosive—the unanalyzed dissatisfaction of the bulk of the American people. That dissatisfaction is not a neat, paragraphed, and numbered indictment. It is more like a huge charge of electricity ready to discharge itself. Conceivably, it could supply the voltage for a thoroughly vital social movement toward a better society. But it could also break to the surface in political upheavals and in devastating conflict between groups in the society."

That is all too urgently true. Unfortunately, business and industry do not alone have the power to solve the massive problems which confront this country. But they can be immensely influential, as Mr. Gardner suggested, in determining what problems the community will seek to solve, and how it should go about solving them. That high order of leadership is still all too rare, and we should all honor it when we see it.

CHARLES C. RANDOLPH
Publisher, *Business Week*

New York, New York

# Contents

# 1

# Industry Involvement

*"Everything is related to everything"*

You hear it in the mayor's office. You hear it in the corporate boardroom. You hear it almost everywhere, in fact, that the so-called "urban crisis" is discussed.

"Business and industry built our cities," says Cleveland's energetic Negro Mayor Carl B. Stokes. "If they are going to be rebuilt, it will take more of that same investment and ingenuity. You can't develop a city without the private sector." As a local leader profoundly concerned about the deterioration of our social and physical environment, Stokes is the first to admit that such a plea for greater business involvement is a 180-degree reversal from local government thinking of a few years ago. In those days, says Stokes, business and government "eyed each other like strange tomcats." Today, he believes, neither business, nor local

1

government, nor society itself can afford not to have business involved in the problems that plague our urban environment.

In New York, Robert Feagles, a senior vice president with Manhattan's First National City Bank, comments upon the same subtle change in society's expectations of business. "Six or eight years ago," says Feagles, "society's demands upon business added up to a simple mandate: pay your taxes, offer reasonable working conditions, provide reasonable compensation, make some charitable donations, produce a product or service which, if not always good, is not necessarily bad. And above all—stay out of the government's business." Now, Feagles notes, society is saying that industry's products and services must pay off in some new and heightened dividend. "Our factories," he observes, "must not contaminate the atmosphere or detract from the landscape. Our products must not litter the roadside. Our employment policies must be broadened to help the disadvantaged minorities. And above all, we must directly involve ourselves in these and all the other social and environmental problems with which the government is deeply concerned."

Those problems grow more serious and more menacing by the day. Racial hatreds coil in our ghettos. Muggers stalk our streets. Traffic is a nightmare. Recreation space is dwindling to the vanishing point. Mountains of solid waste scar our countryside. Water pollution is turning our rivers and lakes into sinkholes. In some cities air pollution almost turns our days into nights. Perhaps even more serious than the problems themselves is what they are doing to our society. Dr. Philip Zimbardo, a research psychologist at Stanford University, feels that urban pressures and frustrations are converting us into a nation of Goths. He points to the sharp increase in murder during the last few years, the 230 violent urban outbreaks since 1964, the string of assassinations, and the estimated 40,000 American youngsters who are beaten and tortured each year by their parents, brothers, or sisters. He further cites an increase in vandalism—often vented on some of our more frustrating institutions. In New York in 1967, he notes, vandals smashed 360,000 pay telephones and 202,712 school windows; they also wreaked another $750,000 worth of havoc on parks and $100,000 worth on the transit system.

*A witches' brew.* Businessmen, of course, will never end vandalism or murder or man's basic inhumanity to man. But they are, for the first time, trying to help reduce some of the root causes of mounting urban unease. They are also moving slowly— if somewhat tentatively—in the direction of what Dr. Charles E. Johnson of the Harvard Business School calls "synethical decision-making." This is a distinctly revolutionary process by which otherwise normal business decisions are governed partly by social, cultural, and environmental considerations. In Chicago, Los Angeles, and Rochester, N.Y., for instance, businessmen joined in the war on crime. In St. Louis, they helped clean up decaying waterfronts. In Portland, Ore., they helped solve a major parking problem. And in almost every big and small city, they are building or renovating slum housing, improving schools, hiring the hardcore unemployed, and rooting out the squalor and blight that—like some painfully impacted tooth—send the fever charts of our cities soaring. What is more, says Donald C. Burnham, president of Westinghouse Electric Corp., industry is being challenged not only to play a key role in these areas, but to "take the lead."

Along the way, business has run into some fiercely forbidding snags, and learned the prickly lesson that, as urbanologist Daniel Patrick Moynihan puts it, "everything is related to everything." It has learned that the so-called "urban crisis" is really a much broader and much murkier witches' brew of crises blended, says David Rockefeller, president of New York's Chase Manhattan Bank, "from all the major ills of our country: inadequate educational systems, hardcore unemployment, hazardous pollution of natural resources, antiquated transportation, shameful housing, insufficient and ineffective public facilities, lack of equal opportunity for all, and a highly dangerous failure of communication between young and old, black and white."

At the same time, business has also run up against a whole new set of questions—all of them loaded. "For example," says Charles Luce, board chairman of New York's Consolidated Edison Co., "should a utility spend $140-million to put 25 miles of transmission lines underground when they can be placed overhead for $12-million? If so, who should pay the added cost: the people who live in the areas where the lines are to be buried and thus benefit directly? All the customers, through rates? Taxpayers? Which taxpayers: local, state, or federal? Suppose a utility operates in a market with an adequate supply of skilled labor. Should it nevertheless spend money to train members of underprivileged groups to raise their levels of opportunity? Should ratepayers or taxpayers bear the cost of the training program? Should a utility spend $2-million extra to make a generating station better looking, and perhaps build a playground next door to it? How deeply should it get into public recreation? Is not its primary duty to provide plentiful low-cost energy?"

*Bread cast upon the waters.*   Many businessmen still shrug off such involvement and the tortuous questions it raises as so much "do-goodism" or charity. They feel, as MIT economist Paul Samuelson puts it, that "the business of business is business" and "under laissez faire, everybody's business [that is, the public weal] is nobody's business."

That may be true in the rare cases where companies are responding purely out of some lofty sense of mission. But increasingly, they are responding to something much more basic: the profit motive. "There is no longer anything to reconcile, if there ever was, between the social conscience and the profit motive," Henry Ford II has said. "Improving the quality of society—investing in better employees and customers for tomorrow—is nothing more than another step in the evolutionary process of taking a more far-sighted view of return on investment." Often, the return is far more immediate. As the president of a major job-training company says trenchantly, if somewhat earthily: "Whenever a human problem is solved, it's always because somebody has found a way to make a buck on it."

By helping to rehabilitate 3,000 apartments in Boston's Roxbury ghetto, for instance, Eastern Gas & Fuel Associates provided better housing for several thousand people—and gained 3,000 gas-using customers. By making traffic studies for San Diego and Salt Lake City, Ford Motor Co. hopes to help untangle traffic jams—and thus sell more cars. In tackling an air pollution problem at its plants, Monsanto Co. not only cleaned up its own air—but developed a profitable new line of pollution abatement equipment.

*Nationwide concern.* By involving itself, business is also responding to stiff public pressures. A poll by Opinion Research Corp. shows that 65% of American stockholders feel business should play an active role in the war on poverty. H. I. Romnes, board chairman of American Telephone & Telegraph Co. (see Chapter 4), considers it a matter of survival. "We must remember," he notes, "that most Americans now live in the cities, and they constitute the great majority of our customers. The problems of the cities, therefore, are our problems, and the future of the cities is our future."

Another survey by the Gallup poll shows that 86% of Americans are also "concerned" about environmental deterioration, and many blame industry. Author Norman Mailer speaks for millions of fed-up fellow New Yorkers when he says, "The only way to end our smog is for citizens to take up muskets, get on barges, go to Jersey, and explode all the factories." On the West Coast, Californians are making the environment a constitutional issue. After picking up 500,000 signatures, a recent petition will go on the state's 1970 ballot, putting "the primary responsibility for eliminating environmental pollution" squarely upon "the manufacturers of pollution producing products and industries which cause pollution in their activities."

## The Fire Next Time

If there are profits and pressures, there are also problems. And nowhere are the problems greater—or the stakes higher—than in the social or ghetto area, industry's biggest single focus of involvement. After the 1967 Detroit riots, black militant Norvel Harrington laid it on the line for the New Detroit Committee—and the nation. To the likes of Henry Ford II, James M. Roche, board chairman of General Motors Corp., and Lynn Townsend, board chairman and chief executive officer of Chrysler Corp., Harrington warned: "If you fat cats don't give us what we want, it won't be our places that are burning down next summer. It'll be yours." Amid Harrington's barrage of four-letter words and tough talk, according to one committee member, GM's Roche twitched and slinked deeper and deeper into his chair. Nearly three years later, the stakes are just as high and the challenge just as great. "This is the one area where business cannot afford to fail," says Dr. Courtney Brown, retired dean of Columbia University's Graduate School of Business. "Yet it is also the one area where business—because of the emotional intangibles involved—will never completely succeed." Consider the plight of the private organizations for social uplift:

*The Urban Coalition,* born out of the ashes of the Detroit riots three years ago, set out to mobilize all major urban institutions and map a coordinated attack on ghetto ills. Today, the coalition has blossomed out to 48 affiliates, organized some laudable programs, and generated a dizzying array of facts, figures, and ephemera. But on both a national and local level, it is beset by factional disputes and proliferating bureaucracies.

The New York Urban Coalition lost four key executives in five months during 1969. The Boston coalition collapsed completely. In Minneapolis, internal squabbles ruptured into the open when one embittered coalition member resigned, calling his local group "just another middle-class social agency of the kind that has failed so miserably for so many years"; the same week, black militants broke up one of the coalition's meetings and declared formation of their own "people's coalition." In Los Angeles, the coalition has trouble just assembling a quorum. In Chicago, no one has yet even formed a coalition—despite the fact that Mayor Richard Daley sits on the national coalition's board of directors.

*The National Alliance of Businessmen,* organized a few months after the Urban Coalition, now has 18,500 member companies, has placed more than 200,000 ghetto residents in jobs, and is shooting for 614,000 placements by June, 1971. However, large companies still dominate the hiring, partly because many small and medium-sized companies are either not committing themselves or simply do not know about the program. On a speaking visit to New York in 1969, NAB President Paul Kayser admitted that he found it "absolutely incredible, the number of people who don't know who we are." Those few small companies that are getting involved often are unequipped to do so. Jack H. Ducate, metropolitan director of the Dallas branch of the NAB, cites the case of a small local firm that hired 20 hard-core unemployed—and lost all 20.

Others claim that the jobs offered are frequently too menial. One of these critics is William Kaufmann, executive director of New York's Coalition JOBS. The product of a merger between the New York branch of the NAB and the New York Urban Coalition's Manpower Task Force, Coalition JOBS aims for fewer, but better, jobs. "It does no good," says Kaufmann, "to take a man who is leaning against a lamppost and lean him against a broom. You have to motivate him."

*Many local groups* are also problem-plagued. Boston's Opportunities Industrialization Center, a three-year-old job training agency, set out in 1969 to raise $900,000. It came up with only $225,000. Of 3,000 greater Boston companies hit for contributions, a scant 90 came up with anything at all, and a mere handful kicked in more than $1,000. The city's teen-age Youth Alliance hoped to drum up $150,000. It raised less than one-third of that. The New Detroit Committee—possibly anticipating some of the same problems—merged its money-raising effort with the local United Fund. In the future, the committee plans to concentrate more on performing a catalytic role and getting others to pick up the bill.

*Reevaluations.*    Such problems are partly the cause, partly the effect, of a broad shake-out in the business commitment. "This was bound to happen," says Louis Winnick, an urban specialist with the Ford Foundation. "A businessman is a pragmatist. If he puts something in one end, he wants to see something else pop out the other end. And in this area you just don't get quick clean results." William Hart, manager of state and urban affairs for General Electric Co., claims the shake-out does not reflect a lessening sense of commitment so much as a growing sense of reality. "You have to go into this field with a full hand of cards," Hart stresses. "You're not just dealing with joblessness. You're also dealing with poor housing, poor schools, lack of training— people caught in an appalling web of frustration and despair. And you have to know what you're up against."

## All in the Motive

Many companies that did not know are quietly easing off the gas. Others that were committed from the first are still committed, and are often juicing up their commitment. Shortly after the Detroit riots, the life insurance industry pledged $1-billion to help rebuild the inner cities. In April, 1969, the industry upped its ante another $1-billion. "The do-gooders come and go in waves," says Francis E. Ferguson, president of Northwestern

Mutual Life Insurance Co. and chairman of the industry's inner-city investment program. "But the person with good, solid economic motives follows through and really makes a program work." The insurance industry's motive: a $60-billion investment in the central cities. The $2-billion inner-city program adds a whole new magnitude to that investment. A typical cross-sampling:

A $3,298,000 bond issue, in which several companies participated, for a 586-bed dormitory and dining facilities at Knoxville College in Knoxville, Tenn.'s core area.

$408,500 to finance Negro ownership, operation, and rehabilitation of four separate apartment buildings in the Boston area.

$5,500,000 to purchase a group of 375 loans by assignment from the Bank of Finance, a Negro bank near the Watts area of Los Angeles.

$6-million to cover the cost of major improvements in a new hospital addition in the heart of Cincinnati's Avondale neighborhood, the scene of 1967 riots.

$170,000 to finance the rehabilitation of a movie theater in the core area of Roxbury, Mass.

$100,000 to provide financial leadership in underwriting the equity capital for New England's first bi-racial bank, located in Dorchester, Mass.

$5,400,000 to finance an industrial plant and electronics and programming institute in Minneapolis to hire and train minority persons.

*Economic trap.* In some cases, insurance companies lowered their rates below the going market. In the private housing field, for instance, Equitable Life Assurance Society, which has pledged a total of $171.4-million to the industry fund, offered interest rates as much as 1% below market. The problem for black home buyers, says Alfred R. Plager, Equitable assistant vice president and head of the company's new Office of Urban Redevelopment, is that they normally have to pay one-third more than whites for comparable housing. "That sets up a vicious cycle which economically traps people," Plager notes. With its inner-city housing loans, Equitable is making it possible for 6,700 families to purchase or refinance their homes, and— where possible—is working through mortgage firms owned or managed by Negroes. "In human values," says Plager, "I don't know how you measure that kind of help. But I know it's a lot."

The satisfactions have led many insurance companies to go beyond their industry pledges. Boston's John Hancock Mutual Life Insurance Co., for instance, pledged a total of $114-million to the industry program. In addition, the company pledged $10-million for construction of low-income housing on city-owned vacant lots, made a major stock purchase in a new bi-racial bank in the city's Roxbury ghetto, and runs a variety of training programs for blacks. Just how far a company should go in trying to solve the urban crisis, says Robert E. Slater, former president of John Hancock, "is a question every top officer of the company is wrestling with. My own opinion is that we should probably go further than we have." One thing to remember, however, "is that you can't expect this thing to be solved overnight. I think more can be done. But much has been done, and is being done."

*A closer look.*    In retailing, Phillips-Van Heusen Corp. and the 3,300-member Menswear Retailers of America have set up a similar industry effort: a $20-million longterm credit pool that has helped some 30 black merchants start up their own clothing stores. Lawrence Phillips, president of Phillips-Van Heusen, says a "realistic goal" for the program would be 500 new stores. "In my own case," says Phillips, "I just wasn't satisfied with making contributions to various organizations, and I think many other businessmen feel the same way." So Phillips decided to plunge in on a closer and more personal level, "where I could watch what was happening and how it was happening." The program goes beyond simply supplying credit. Says Roy G. Sheldon, former president of MRA and one of the principal organizers of the credit pool: "Someone has to guide this new businessman in selecting a profitable location, deciding on merchandise lines, selecting fixtures, negotiating leases, getting adequate insurance, coordinating other financing, and attempting to perform an education job in a matter of weeks that normally would take a number of years."

One typical recipient of industry help is Rufus Butler, owner of Mr. B's Men's Shop in Portland, Ore. He is receiving assistance from Levi Strauss & Co. (see Chapter 3). "I wrote 'em," Butler recalls, speaking of Strauss, "that I didn't know what extended credit was but that we sure needed it. Next thing, their local Levi Strauss man was here saying if he didn't do business with me, his boss would probably fire him." The first store to open under the industry program—New York's Le Mans Haberdashers, Inc., located on Manhattan's Upper West Side—reports business is flourishing after the first year's operation. "Our first Christmas," says Kermith Morgan, the dapper president of Le Mans, "we had black customers come in from Newark, Connecticut, and all the New York City boroughs." This was largely the result of widespread newspaper and television publicity about the store.

## Creating Values as Well as Profits

Some businessmen have become literally one-man urban renewal programs. One of these is Sam E. Wyly, youthful (35), soft-spoken board chairman of the fastgrowing University Computing Co. of Dallas, Tex. Wyly recently opened a new data preparation center in El Paso, where 100 previously unemployed Mexican-American women are operating key-tape conversion equipment. At Riverton, Wyo., the company is hiring Shoshone and Arapahoe Indians to produce typewriter terminals for use in computer timesharing. The Sam Wyly Foundation, established in 1968, has invested $500,000 in minority business enterprises, ranging from a plastics manufacturing operation and real estate ventures to a transportation company that takes ghetto workers to and from their jobs. The foundation has also made a $54,000 grant to a black-managed advisory business called Ventures Advisors. Wyly's biggest single project, however, may result in the Lazarus-like revival of an entire town: the all-black community of Boley, Okla.

*A brighter future.* A flyspeck in the barren, 100-mi. wasteland stretching between Oklahoma City and Tulsa, Boley is one of the poorest towns in the most poverty-stricken section of the state. Its population has plummeted from 4,000 in 1900 to 600, and its median income is down to a dismal $1,300. In 1968, however, things began to look up. Bonanza International, Inc., a nationwide steakhouse chain owned by University Computing, started planning a new chain of barbecue restaurants and began dickering for a patented cooker produced by Boley's one and only industrial employer—M. W. Lee Mfg. Co. Charles C. Green, now regional director of the Dept. of Health, Education, and Welfare in Dallas, was then president of Bonanza. When the negotiations began dragging out, Green was on the verge of tossing in the towel. "I felt the size of the Lee company didn't warrant the management time we were spending on it," Green recalls. "I said 'let's forget it.' But Sam sent back word saying, 'Let's try again.'"

The decision to continue, Wyly recalls, was not made out of any high-blown altruism. "Charles Green and his team," Wyly notes, "were thinking in terms of new jobs and new opportunities as well as profits. But the company is not in the charity business or the business of losing stockholders' money. If we were interested, it had to be a sound business proposition that would allow individuals to create values. Otherwise, the venture would fold up and no good would come of it for Boley or the company."

In a last ditch effort to reach agreement, Green and his wife drove from Dallas to Boley one Sunday afternoon in the summer of 1968, visited the Lee family, and at last closed the deal. Bonanza agreed to buy Lee Mfg. for $15,000 in cash and 5,000 Bonanza shares—which tripled in value from $6.50 to $19 a share shortly afterward when Bonanza went public. As a result of the deal, Boley is now getting a new Lee plant and at least 50 new jobs. In addition, University Computing plans to produce the frames for its peripheral computer equipment in Boley, and a furniture plant is also under consideration.

*"Whatever is necessary."* Mills B. Lane, Jr., president of Georgia's powerful Citizens and Southern National Bank, is another businessman who has done big things in a big way. A bit of a local legend, Lane wears ties inscribed "It's a wonderful world," booms the same message to visitors and phone-callers, and once tethered sheep in his main downtown branch to stimulate interest in sheep-grazing. His casual dress, fizzy personality, relentless optimism, and attention-grabbing antics guaranteed that when he decided to involve his bank in social problems, the effort would come clearly stamped with his own personal style. Since June, 1968, Lane and his bank have invested $2.5-million in Savannah's slums. Operating through a subsidiary called Community Development Corp., Lane has organized a huge trash cleanup, financed 28 new businesses, the purchase of 75 new homes, the renovation of 1,000 others, and the construction of a new slum-area playground. In 1969, Lane broadened his program to 11 other Georgia cities—all served by his bank.

In the first year, loans were all "high-risk." None were defaulted. "We have had to extend some of the payments for 30 days, but no one has missed one yet," says C&S director of Community Development Robert F. Clayton. Several of the high-risk borrowers are even paid up far in advance. Ralph Lipsey, who received such a loan and opened the first Negro auto dealership in Savannah, is thriving. He was even offered the Renault and Jeep franchises. The CDC has also financed a grocery store bought by a Negro bread salesman from a white, a combination beauty and barber shop, a dry cleaning plant, a record and music store, and several restaurants. One of the restaurants, Jimmy Washington's Soul Foods, has done so well that it went looking for space to expand.

Part of the success of the loan program lies in Lane's approach to the borrower. "We teach a man how to run a business," he says. "We don't just lend him money and turn him loose." To keep the program going, Lane has personally pledged "whatever is necessary to do the job."

*More than money.* In some cases, what it takes is not so much money as hard business savvy and resourcefulness. Witness Philadelphia's Smith Kline & French Laboratories, which has its headquarters immediately adjacent to a squalid 20-block ghetto, housing 15,000 of the city's most disadvantaged and despairing inhabitants. "They are the lowest on the totem pole," says one SK&F executive. "The birth rate is higher than Hong Kong, and one-third are illegitimate." After years of contributing to private welfare agencies that promised to help the neighborhood, SK&F decided in 1966 to become more directly involved with its neighbors.

To encourage a local developer to spruce up the area's housing, SK&F covered 40% of the interest on his renovation loans. By the end of 1969, he had renovated 70 large homes and converted them into 200 modern, low-cost apartments. The cost to SK&F: only $4,000. SK&F also helped the neighborhood pick up a big, century-old limestone mansion and convert it into a community center at only a fraction of the normal cost. It pulled off this sleight-of-hand by helping arrange first and second mortgages, plus longterm lease commitments from several tenants. For another $6,000, the company converted part of its parking lot into a lighted playground for evening and weekend use.

SK&F gets additional mileage out of a neighborhood information services center, set up in an abandoned church three blocks from SK&F's office. SK&F reasoned that there was no shortage of agencies to help people, but that many people were unable, afraid, or simply ignorant of how to get the available aid. On a budget of $70,000, the center has helped these people solve the problems that keep them from feeling like useful citizens—housing, medical treatment, employment, rat control, even creating a family budget. "The contribution we are making," says President Thomas M. Rauch, "isn't the dollars we spend. It's the know-how. Government can outspend us, but it can't out-talent us."

## The Frustrations Pile Up

Another quality just as important is patience—especially in the one area where industry is applying most of its muscle: job training. Equitable Life Assurance Society began a job training program for high school dropouts in 1962. Within six months, 45% of its dropouts had dropped out. Turnover for the year stood at 67%—more than three times that of the company as a whole. "It didn't take us long to learn," one Equitable vice president recalls, "that dropouts lived in a world outside our experience." Within a month after the company hired one dropout, for instance, he disappeared. "People who answered his telephone said they didn't know him," Equitable's manpower vice president recalls. "A letter sent to him was returned as undeliverable. His parents could not be located. Initially, no one in his neighborhood could be found who would admit they knew where or who he was. At last an address was given to us—an address that turned out to be a local hospital. We found him there dying of cancer."

*New definition.* When Chrysler Corp. began hiring the hardcore unemployed, Chrysler's President Virgil Boyd thought he knew what "hardcore" meant. "I was wrong," he admits.

"Hardcore refers not to those without steady jobs, but those who are not equipped for any job. Not the unemployed, but the unemployable—those who are unable to fill out even a simple job application." Some of Chrysler's applicants signed on for job training, then never showed up. Others who did report were notoriously late. As Chrysler registered those who did report, it found that many of them had never been counted in a census, had no social security number, had never registered to vote, and belonged to no organizations of any kind. "In most of the accepted senses," Boyd says, "they really didn't even exist."

In Caterpillar Tractor Co.'s job training program, one trainee was chronically late because he could not read the route signs on city buses. A trainee at another company came from a rural area where no one worked on rainy days; so on his new job he simply stayed home when it rained. At Hallmark Cards, Inc., in Kansas City, another disadvantaged employee—a woman—had to be helped out financially because her furniture was repossessed, and she and her children were sleeping on the floor. During its first venture into training the hardcore, Eastman Kodak Co. assigned some of its best craftsmen as instructors. "After a while," says Vice President Frederic S. Welsh, "we made a discovery. The instructors were not teaching tools and tolerances. They were teaching reading, writing, and arithmetic." Many of the hardcore unemployed are so lacking in education, adds J. H. Tinsley, director of public affairs at Warner & Swasey Co., that they have to be taught even how to learn.

*Stark profile.*   From his experience in working with the disadvantaged, Stephen Keating, president of Honeywell, Inc., draws a stark portrait of the damp and subterranean world of the ghetto. "Among disadvantaged youths of 18," he says, "probably not more than 25% have lived with both parents all their lives. In their homes there is little tradition of work, of education, of family stability, community responsibility, or individual achievement." In fact, he adds, the average middle-class American probably shares more in common with his counterpart in France or Japan than with the disadvantaged family living only a few blocks away. "Young people who never finished high school," Keating observes, "come into employment offices and apply for jobs as salesmen or technicians. They seem to have no idea of the training such jobs require or how people ready themselves for these assignments."

A Honeywell interviewer tells the story of offering a young, disadvantaged youth a job, and explaining that the shift started at 8 a.m. The applicant replied, without a trace of rancor or sarcasm: "I don't get up that early"—and out the door he went.

*Shift in focus.* To prepare the disadvantaged for the work-a-day world, many companies are even going into the classroom. Some companies sponsor "street academies" to help high school students and dropouts complete their studies and go on to college. In Cleveland's Hough area, where unemployment runs 15.5%—one of the highest inner-city unemployment rates in the country—GE donated a $5-million, 200,000-sq.-ft. building to the local school system, and helped set up a "school-factory" to educate and train high school dropouts. By the end of 1969, the school-factory had trained and placed more than 300 workers.

In Detroit, Chrysler "adopted" one of the area's largest and toughest inner-city high schools. "Too often in the past," says Lynn Townsend, board chairman and chief executive officer at Chrysler, "education has been designed to prepare young people for college." Chrysler re-focused—with encouraging results—on the great masses who never make it to college. The company created special courses in clerical work and other basic business skills; it also installed an automobile service training center, complete with a one-ton crane, floor hoists, an engine analyzer, brake lab equipment, air tools, and all the other appurtenances of a well-stocked service station.

To add a little incentive, Boron Oil Co. agreed to place advanced shop students in related jobs outside school. Boron and Chrysler also set up a savings plan at a local black-owned bank to encourage the students to salt away at least 10% of their wages every week. As seed money, each company kicked $5 into every account.

Across town, Michigan Bell Telephone Co. formed a similar partnership, and even fashioned a remedial summer program for 60 students. Recalls Edward N. Hodges III, Michigan Bell's employment supervisor, guiding godfather behind the "adoption," and a Negro who came from a broken home himself: "We told the summer school teachers, 'Be as innovative as you want. You're not under the auspices of the board of education.' " In the English class, students read such books as Claude Brown's incendiary *Manchild in the Promised Land,* and wrote "some rather raw" short stories. In math, the instructor taught fractions by inventing a card game. After six weeks, the students boosted their achievement scores as much as two or three years. "I don't think we taught the kids that much," Hodges feels. "I think they were just turned on."

*Drop in requirements.* As part of their more liberalized job-hiring programs, some companies are simply lowering their educational requirements. Others are overlooking minor police records. Several are even hiring those hardest of the hardcore— ex-convicts. With the hearty approval of state prison authorities, the Electronic Computer Programming Institute, a nationwide chain of 91 schools, has set up prison training programs in California, Pennsylvania, Ohio, and New York, and has trained and placed more than 40 inmates as computer programmers. One Sing Sing trainee, Rego A. ——— a 37-year-old bachelor who served 20 months of a 2½- to 5-year sentence—received a job straight out of prison with a Manhattan firm. The company's data-processing manager had been opposed at first. "I have enough problems," he said, "without taking on a jail-bird." But he finally agreed, and Rego submitted to a tough 4½-hour examination. He scored almost perfect results, and the manager hired him on the spot at $125 a week.

Among the staunchest boosters of such programs is Sen. Jacob Javits (R–N.Y.). "More than four-fifths of all prisoners over age 25 have not completed high school," he says. "In the population as a whole, the percentage is 55%. In the general population, 39% are employed as service workers, laborers, and in other low-level and low-paid jobs. In the prison population, 77% fit into these lowest categories of job skills and income. To the extent that poor educational achievement and poor job skills are directly related to crime rates, the correctional process offers a major opportunity to break the wasteful cycle through education and job training programs."

## Bid for Black Ownership

Many black moderates and militants insist that all this job preparation and training is not the answer at all. "Hell," says one black militant in Harlem, "if jobs were the problem, there would never have been a Detroit riot." They call for more black ownership of ghetto businesses—especially of the 25 or 30 white-owned plants that industry has sprinkled through the ghetto to provide jobs. Most of these plants are already black-run, and some are scheduled to revert to community ownership once they get on their feet. So far, performance is spotty.

■ In Los Angeles, Watts Mfg. Co., which may turn its first profit in 1969, remains financially dependent on its parent company, Aerojet-General Corp. Toward the end of 1969, Aerojet had poured nearly $2-million into the company. Aerojet Executive Vice President L. W. Mullane, who serves as Watts Mfg.'s board chairman, says one difficulty is finding employees willing to accept promotion. "Some people don't want to boss their friends," says Mullane, and managerial skills among blacks are not abundant. "If we had it to do over again," he feels, "we would open a training school for supervisors the same day we start a training school for the rank and file."

■ In Brooklyn's Bedford-Stuyvesant section, the International Business Machines Corp. plant is meeting production schedules—but overall efficiency and performance continue below that of other IBM plants.

■ In Boston, EG&G, Inc.'s Roxbury sheet metal plant is expected to lose up to $300,000 in 1969—three times what had originally been expected. After dumping the plant's black management early in the year, EG&G executives now claim they are slowly turning the plant around.

■ In Cleveland, two other black-managed plants—one owned by Warner & Swasey, the other supported by Harris-Intertype Corp.—are troubled by "incredible ineptitude," "books you wouldn't believe" and "unbelievable work practices," insiders say.

*Partnerships.* Partly because of such problems, Eastman Kodak decided against opening an inner-city plant. Instead, it rallied local business and formed the Rochester Business Opportunities Corp. Since its founding in 1968, RBOC has funnelled nearly $2-million into 47 inner-city businesses, and considerably improved the prospects of the city's black businessman. Among those helped was James A. Greene, who started a black beauty products business in 1963, and had been limping along—hand to mouth—for several years. "When I started up," Greene recalls, "banks just weren't giving money to Negro business. Now if you were going to buy a Cadillac, you could get all the money you wanted. But to go into business? No." Then after the Rochester riots of 1964, the banks finally loosened up—a little. In 1965 Greene received a $1,000 loan from Marine Midland Trust Co.

He did not really get his financial footing, however, until RBOC came into existence and granted him an $8,000 loan.

One local militant Negro group warmed to the RBOC idea so much that it took a rare step: it went into business with industry. Working with Xerox Corp. and RBOC, the militant group—called FIGHT—set up an inner-city plant for manufacturing transformers and metal stampings.

Several other companies are helping black capitalists crowbar their way into fields long closed off to them—most notably, the construction industry. General Motors recently made a $1.1-million interest-free loan to a black development group building 500 low-income housing units. In rehabilitating two low-income apartment buildings in Cleveland, Warner & Swasey picked a company made up of ten skilled Negro tradesmen. To build its plant in Boston's Roxbury section, Avco Corp. hired eight black contractors, and one of them, in turn, went out and hired 15 inexperienced ghetto residents rather than regular union men. To train his new unskilled employees, contractor Lawrence James designed a three-week course, including lectures on money management by the president of a local ghetto bank, building trade licenses by an assistant from the mayor's office, personal protection by an insurance agent, and personal legal matters by an attorney. "Eventually," James enthuses, "we'll be training carpenters, electricians, plumbers, and steel erectors."

*Inevitable control.*    A far newer wrinkle is the "black conglomerate," the community organization that tries—usually with white financing—to do a smattering of everything. "This is what black economic development must inevitably come down to," says Donald Simmons, an ebullient, articulate economist and executive director of the Harlem Commonwealth Council. "Only by having a broad-based community organization that controls the capital instruments of the community can the black man ever pull himself up."

Right now, Harlem—like most other ghettos—suffers from a situation in which 80% of its 6,000 retail and manufacturing companies are owned and managed by white businessmen who live outside the ghetto. Every night after work, they drain away the area's precious capital—the lifeblood of a healthy economy. This constant hemorrhaging debilitates the ghetto. With a $400,000 research and development grant from the Office of Economic Opportunity, economic experts at New York's Columbia University and the New School for Social Research recently completed an intensive study of the Harlem economy, and decided that Harlem could not really stand on its own feet economically. Columbia's Stanislaw Wellisz, the project coordinator, felt that Harlem lacked the physical space for any ambitious industrial development. The New School's Thomas Vietorisz, an MIT-trained economist, concluded that because opportunities were limited for profitable investment, the ghetto was incapable of generating anywhere near the number of jobs it needed to become self-sufficient. "It is much easier to find ghetto investments that yield only 1% or 2% profit than it is to find the 10% to 15% yield that businessmen are accustomed to getting," says Vietorisz. He thinks that Harlem's economic future lies in development of what he calls "greenhouse industries" that justify themselves not by the profits they produce, but by the social benefits they generate.

To HCC's Simmons and other black power advocates, these views are anathema, since they mean that the ghetto's economy will always be dependent on white society—either for funds to operate these greenhouse industries, or for jobs that the ghetto could not provide for itself. "The only way we can stop being a colony," the HCC executive director insists, "is to form profit-making enterprises." The HCC conglomerate is still little more than a gleam in Simmons' eye. It consists of a Singer Sewing Machine shop and a $500,000 metals foundry. But HCC is in the process of creating a finance company, two shoe stores, a data-processing company, a fleet of taxicabs, and an automotive diagnostic center. It is also negotiating to buy two large Harlem supermarkets and set up nine HCC-owned service stations.

*Doing as whites do.* Another ripple on this new wave is James E. Hurt, Jr., a black entrepreneur in St. Louis. "Negroes are living in a profit-making society without making profits," he says. "It's not important how many people we put to work, it's profits. White people built this country by forming corporations and combining their resources. The only way for Negroes to make it in this society is for them to do what white people have done." Hurt has been the driving force in a diverse array of Negro businesses, ranging from a new supermarket in the heart of the St. Louis ghetto to a community newspaper and housing for the poor. In the process, his Employee's Loan and Investment Co., which he inherited from his father, has expanded its assets from $35,000 to $1.1-million.

The showpiece of Hurt's efforts is his Central City Foods, Inc., which is capitalized with 20,000 shares sold at $10 each to 2,000 people in the ghetto. The idea for the supermarket grew out of weekly meetings which Hurt holds with a group of ministers to discuss the black community's problems. When the decision was made to build the supermarket, the ministers spread the word among their congregations that they could buy a piece of the action—at $10 a share. At the same time, Hurt formed Vanguard Redevelopment Corp. and Vanguard Bond & Mortgage Corp. to bid on a parcel of urban renewal land, then to put up the building. Boatmen's National Bank of St. Louis and First National Bank in St. Louis supplied loans, and Hurt picked up a $228,000 mortgage from General American Life Insurance Co. From General Grocer Co. came advice on site selection, supermarket layout and design, hiring and testing practices, and merchandise planning.

## The Value of Communication
## and Dialogue

In Philadelphia, Rev. Leon H. Sullivan hopes to do on a national
scale what St. Louis' Hurt and New York's Simmons are doing on
a local level. Converting his Baptist congregation into a holding
company, Sullivan has formed a dress manufacturing operation,
the country's first black-owned and -operated aerospace firm, a
nationwide chain of 80 job-training schools, and the first of what
Sullivan hopes will be a nationwide chain of black-operated
shopping centers. Since 1964, more than 50,000 people, mostly
unemployed and underemployed blacks, have taken courses at
Sullivan's training centers. His five Philadelphia centers alone
claim they have placed some 90% of their more than 7,000 gradu-
ates directly into jobs, and the local chamber of commerce
estimates that Sullivan's overall programs have pumped $30-mil-
lion into the city's economy.

As actual profit-making enterprises, however, none of Sullivan's ventures is a thumping financial success. In fact, many of
Sullivan's critics claim that his companies succeed in almost direct proportion to his distance from them. For instance, his
aerospace company, which was launched with a ratio of about
two skilled production workers to every unskilled trainee, is having troubles. GE, which supplied the technical expertise to get
the company going, came back in during 1969, and for all intents
and purposes was running the company. It will move out again
when the company stabilizes.

Perhaps the greater measure of Sullivan's talent is that he has
managed to build a working dialogue with white industry. The
result is that hundreds of businessmen now channel their social
and economic good works through him, and some 30 companies—including IBM, GE, Coca-Cola Co., and Kaiser Industries, Inc.—serve on the National Advisory Council of Sullivan's
Opportunities Industrialization Centers, Inc.

Such an organization also builds a dialogue with the black community—something few white organizations or individual companies have been able to do. One reason the black man will listen to Sullivan: He minces no words. He once appeared on a local television show with officers of a Philadelphia bank that had been one of his first financial backers. When the bank officials tried to ballyhoo their financial role in Sullivan's operations, he cut them off. Black folks, he said, had anted up the front money to get the loan. Sullivan had not asked the bank for any favors. He went there with money in hand and was paying interest like any other borrower. Similarly, when Candidate Nixon visited Sullivan's shopping center in 1968 and tried to make some political hay out of his commitment to black capitalism, Sullivan answered that there was no option. The country had to generate some new positive programs—or else. Recalls one bystander: "I can still see Sullivan standing head and shoulders over Nixon, taking Nixon's thunder. Sullivan wasn't trying to blackmail Nixon. He was just telling it the way it was."

*Long wait.* Among white businessmen, all the best intentions in the world could not establish the kind of rapport that Sullivan has built up with the black community. Besides its work with Sullivan in Philadelphia, for instance, GE also wanted to pitch in and help the Mantua Industrial Development Corp. in the neighboring town of Mantua. MIDC is buying and developing a string of small businesses that will be black-run and -managed, and also plans to build what is believed to be the country's first black industrial park, to be located near Philadelphia International Airport. GE wanted to help. "But it took a full ten months," says one weary GE community relations man, "until any Mantuan leaders even returned our phone calls."

Or consider New York's Chase Manhattan Bank, which recognized the problem early and got involved. Chase Manhattan's David Rockefeller recalls the story of a Chase representative who visited nearly 300 retailers in Harlem, trying to find out what additional services the bank could provide for the small businessman. "Almost everywhere he went," says Rockefeller, "he was viewed with suspicion." Finally, the Chase man took to keeping the flaps of his coat open to show he was not carrying a gun. He also had to begin some visits by explaining that he was not a policeman, a tax collector, a social worker, or a hold-up man.

*Loners.*   Because of such suspicions, many black capitalists try to go it completely alone—and learn the hard way. For instance, there is Los Angeles' Green Power Foundation, organized in 1967 by black businessman Norman Hodges. Says H. C. McClellan, executive director of the city's Council for Merit Employment, Training, and Research: "Hodges came in here with a lot of charisma and the idea of the Watts Walloper, a baseball bat. We recommended a feasibility study. They ignored it, and lost $150,000." An umbrella organization set up to spawn black businesses, Green Power now has seven companies. The original company has turned from baseball bats to furniture, sandboxes, and picnic tables. Other subsidiaries include a trucking company, a small garment manufacturing operation, and a gas station. Hodges says the foundation will turn the corner financially by the end of 1969—this time with the counseling of volunteers from white industry.

One black capitalist who has made it almost entirely on his own is Al Hollingsworth, president of Sheet Plant Corp., a highly successful Los Angeles box company. "I won't open my books to whites," say Hollingsworth. "And I'm negative to coddling by big businessmen who want to help us avoid the bumps inherent in a capitalist system. We have the ability to look equally at success and failure. We make mistakes like everyone else." If there is any problem, he says, "it's not knowing where to go for help"— or more specifically, financial aid. Hollingsworth feels that white financial help carries too many strings. He also feels that white business should be prejudiced and buy from blacks until black business is a going concern. "Business needs business to prosper.

Black capitalists don't regard financial help with disfavor—except when whites throw out a bone and say your price must be lower."

*Tally-card.* So how does the scoresheet add up? How are black capitalists doing? "We're moving," says James Shorter, head of the Cleveland office of the Black Economic Union. "It's not what it should be, but it's moving. We're getting more cooperation from the lending institutions." In California, for instance, a group of seven banks recently banded together and created a $2-million fund for direct loans to promising minority ventures, without SBA guarantees and at interest rates only slightly above prime. Says Melvin C. Yocum, president of the consortium's "Opportunity through Ownership" program: "The standards for success are the same as for any business, but the standards for judging the applicant's track record are different. No appreciable accumulation of net worth is required, no collateral." In Philadelphia, First Pennsylvania Banking and Trust Co. was one of the first banks in the country to commit itself to a special loan program for black businessmen. Its "soft loan" program is now in its fourth year, and over $2-million has been invested in black-run companies.

## Salvaging the Downtown Area

In most cities, the dark mood and decay of the ghettos have spread like some inexorable malignancy into adjacent downtown areas. For years, many companies responded by simply packing up and decamping to the suburbs, thus draining away precious tax revenues. Increasingly, however, many downtown companies are now sticking fast, and trying to breathe new life into their moribund neighborhoods. The decision to stay is not always easy. "Economics have a lot to do with it," says Harry B. Warner, president of B. F. Goodrich Co. "But if the cost of renovating and rehabilitating is about the same as starting up in a new location, the decision to stay in a given community is fairly easy"—if only because companies today tend to get more involved with their communities and build closer ties.

As a company that opted to stay, B. F. Goodrich is contributing $3.5-million in seed money toward a $42-million industrial, commercial, and residential complex going up in the neighborhood bordering its Akron headquarters. Campbell Soup Co., Radio Corp. of America, Boise Cascade Corp., and Leon N. Weiner & Associates, Inc., will break ground in 1970 on a $100-million facelifting for downtown Camden, N. J. In downtown Brooklyn, New York City's second busiest retail hub after Manhattan's Herald Square, a group of businessmen and local officials plan a major $500-million remodelling job that will include new office buildings, department stores, and apartment houses interconnected by an underground network of pedestrian passages. Similar efforts are underway in many other cities, ranging from Cincinnati and St. Louis to Niagara Falls, N. Y. (see Chapter 2).

*Atlanta's example.* Without doubt, one of the biggest single downtown renovations is taking place in Atlanta. In the late 1950s, Atlanta was a big, slumbering Southern city where lethargy hung in the air like Spanish moss. Then in 1961, the chamber of commerce kicked off "Forward Atlanta"—a brass-band campaign to lure more business and industry to the city. And slowly but perceptibly, Atlanta began to snap out of its torpor. To get things rolling, the chamber asked the public for $1,500,000. Business immediately pledged $1-million, and 600 volunteers raised the rest. Since then, Atlanta has averaged 27,000 new jobs a year, and more than $1.5-billion worth of new construction has sprouted into the skyline. As part of the city's new spirit, Atlanta went after the franchise of the Milwaukee Braves, and began building an $18-million stadium before a bond issue was approved and even before the Braves had signed a contract agreeing to relocate.

Among the leaders in the city's revival is Atlanta entrepreneur-architect John Portman, Jr., of John Portman & Associates.

His $100-million "Peachtree Center," literally a city within a city, includes a 2-million sq.-ft. Merchandise Mart, three towering office buildings, restaurants, and one of the most striking hotels in the country—the Regency Hyatt House, which features glass-bubble elevators and a lobby courtyard that looks up to a cavernous, 24-story skylight.

"I follow Gertrude Stein's great statement: 'Simplify, simplify,' " says Portman. "Stay with the simple. Work within this framework, let things happen naturally, and realize that people innately desire certain things in buildings—warmth, order, variety." The challenge in revitalizing downtown areas, as Portman sees it: "How do we take little islands within a city—little islands called blocks, which were created during the horse-and-buggy days—and make them able to solve the needs of our modern city and our modern society, and meet the needs of the future?" Portman and other planners have laid out some guidelines. "We must make it easy," he feels, "for people to get to the core. We must make it easy for them to park there. We must make it convenient, pleasant, and attractive to do business in. We must find ways of separating people from vehicular traffic." In order to save the core, he adds, "we must be able to replan and reshape our core, and to do this it may be necessary to close some streets, cross some with bridges or aerial walkways, even go beneath them with tunnels."

*Below-ground.*   Some other Atlanta businessmen are already going beneath the streets—but not to build tunnels. They are doing below ground what Portman and other businessmen are doing above—rebuilding. In a quirk of downtown development, vast sections of Atlanta were sealed over toward the end of the 1800s, leaving some of the old, lower street levels relatively untouched by the 1900s. So a group of private investors has undertaken a four-block subterranean restoration called "Underground Atlanta" and are recreating an historic, turn-of-the-century setting of shops and nightclubs, complete with gaslights, grillworks, and gleaming stained-glass windows. In the first full year of operation in 1973, Underground Atlanta anticipates more than 4-million visitors and $25-million worth of business.

Former Atlanta Mayor Ivan Allen, Jr., feels that such business involvement is "Atlanta's secret for being a great city. Unless you have this kind of support, your really have a sterile government and community."

Progress, however, has brought problems—or as the city's late publisher, Ralph McGill, once cracked: "The fleas come with the dog." And the peskiest flea of all is the city's traffic mess. Many of the city's highways carry three times the traffic they were designed for, and traffic inches along at agonizing, funeral-procession speeds. Some suburbanites spend two hours a day commuting 15 or 20 miles. To head off the threat this poses for downtown business, Atlanta merchants threw their support behind a proposed rapid transit system, and Richard Rich, chairman of Rich's, Inc., Atlanta's big department store, chaired the Metropolitan Atlanta Rapid Transit Authority. But in November, 1968, the voters, already overburdened with taxes, roundly defeated the system.

*Mass transit pitch.*   In the half-dozen other cities where rapid transit systems have been proposed, businessmen are similarly trying to drum up support. They are also backing plans for improvement and expansion of existing systems—improvements long overdue. As President Nixon put it in 1969 when he asked Congress for $10-billion in mass transit aid: "Transit fares have tripled since 1945; the number of passengers has decreased to one-third the level of that year. Transit industry profits before taxes have declined from $313-million in 1945 to $25-million in 1967. In recent years 235 bus and subway companies have gone out of business. The remaining transit companies have progressively deteriorated. Today they give their riders fewer runs, older cars, and less service." Urban planners estimate that 35 new systems will be needed over the next decade, and a jump in total mass transit investment from today's $4.5-billion to $15-billion.

Some of the improvements are already on the way—and stirring plenty of activity among manufacturers. To handle its expanding mass-transit business, GE recently set up a special Transit Systems Dept., and over the last two years has supplied propulsion equipment for more than 900 cars on five systems—a 50% spurt over the preceding two years. Under a contract funded by the U.S. Dept. of Transportation, GE has also designed an experimental, air-cushion train for high-speed, inter-city transit. The 300-mph train would travel on a track and could be in passenger service, GE claims, as early as 1975. Westinghouse is also shooting off sparks. Its research engineers have designed a two-passenger electric scat-about for short-hop city driving, and an elevated, computerized "Transit Expressway" train featuring rubber-tired cars for smoother riding. In the summer of 1969, the company's Transportation Division picked up its biggest contract yet—one covering the computerized controls for San Francisco's sleek, $1.2-billion Bay Area Rapid Transit (BART). The prime contractor for BART, Rohr Corp., is one of many new companies rushing into the market. A sophisticated aerospace firm whose usual line of work is producing jet engine assemblies and giant antennas for NASA and Comsat, Rohr expects to double its total volume to $500-million by 1975. "And a substantial part of that increase," says Rohr President Burt F. Raynes, "will come from the mass-transportation market."

## The Public and Pollution: a New Sense of Urgency

More efficient mass transit would not only help clean up traffic jams. It would also clean up air pollution caused by traffic jams. And in the end, that might be one of industry's biggest contributions at a time when it is under mounting pressure to protect the environment.

*Policy slack.* In 1964, California allowed new cars bought in that state to spew out as much as 900 parts of hydrocarbons

per million parts of exhaust gases. In 1969, the law permitted
only 275 ppm and in 1970, that will drop to 120 ppm. Even now
in California, legislators, pollution control officials, and the man
in the street generally feel that Detroit is not doing enough. Says
C. G. Hass, the state's chief of vehicle emission control: "On the
level of technology, Detroit has been cooperating recently, but
on the policy level, no." Detroit is finally meeting California
standards, in other words, but it fought—and still fights—imple-
mentation of new standards. The reason, thinks Charles Morris,
an engineer working on a smog device for Chromalloy American
Corp., is that Detroit does not sense the critical situation—or the
public mood—within Los Angeles. Morris has worked closely
with Detroit engineers and says, "I sympathize with them. But
where Detroit engineers and I differ is in the sense of urgency.
They don't have to breathe the stuff every day like my family
and I do. I don't care who solves the problem, but someone
must." So barbed is the public feeling in California, in fact, that
a bill to ban the sale of new internal combustion vehicles after
1975 passed the State Senate in 1969, and will be reintroduced
in 1970. On the next vote, it is given an outside chance of passing
both the Senate and the Assembly.

So far, no other states have moved as forcefully against auto-
makers. But the federal government is expected to impose the
same stiff emission standards on cars, and is also talking a
tougher line on pollution control in general. Toward the end of
1969, for instance, U.S. Steel Corp., Republic Steel Corp., Jones
& Laughlin Steel Corp., Interlake Steel Corp., Eagle-Picher Industries, Inc., and the city of Toledo were all on federal notice
to clean up their water pollution or face prosecution. The government plans to move on other polluters along the Savannah
and Passaic Rivers.

*Appropriations gap.*    To help keep things moving, President
Nixon has backed up his Cabinet-level Environmental Quality
Council with a Citizens Advisory Committee on Environmental
Quality, headed by New York's Laurance Rockefeller of the

Rockefeller Brothers Fund. As its first order of business, Rockefeller's committee voiced a polite, but emphatic, criticism of past federal environmental efforts.

The committee listed the following gaps between Congressional authorizations and actual appropriations since fiscal 1965: $2.6-billion in water pollution control grants to states, $171.5-million in the Land & Water Conservation Fund, $193.9-million in air pollution control, nearly $50-million in solid waste management, and $193.8-million in highway beautification. "The justification for these programs still exists," the committee stressed, "and if anything, the problems are more serious today than ever."

*National goals.* Tighter laws are also on the way. Toward the end of 1969, Congress was considering a bill introduced by Senator Edmund Muskie (D.–Me.) that would set up an office of environmental quality, lay out specific national environmental goals, and tailor federal efforts to those goals. Another bill, introduced by Senator Henry Jackson (D.–Wash.), would go further and require Congress and every federal agency to interpret all federal laws and regulations in terms of what they might mean to the environment. "This means," says Jackson, "that the Atomic Energy Commission, the Bureau of Public Works, the Federal Aviation Administration, and a host of other agencies can no longer say they do not have the mandate to give substantive attention to environmental values. It means that a primary concern of all their activities will be not simply the 'preservation' of environmental values, but the positive 'enhancement' of environmental values."

As the pressures grow, businessmen are slowly—if reluctantly—stepping up their anti-pollution efforts. "They moan and gripe," says Lewis C. Green, chairman of the Missouri Air Pollution Control Administration. "But in the end, they comply."

Part of the problem is the mind-boggling complexity of pollution and the absence of any large body of knowledge on it. At this stage, says M. V. Anthony, Stauffer Chemical Co.'s director of pollution control, "we have done little more than identify the problems. We lack medical and biological data on the effects of pollution, and we know little about the fate of pollutants in the atmosphere, in water, or in the soil." There is the added hitch, says Leo J. Weaver, group manager of Monsanto Co.'s Environmental Control Enterprise, that pollution problems are interrelated. "The solving of one type," Weaver notes, "often creates another."

Take a worn-out automobile that has been poisoning the atmosphere for years. Burn it, and it still pollutes the air. Bury it, and it pollutes the soil. Drown it, and it pollutes the water. Leave it, and it pollutes the landscape. Austin N. Heller, New York City's air resources commissioner, cites a case in point: recent reductions of sulfur dioxide in the city's air were accompanied by a corresponding increase—through photochemical reactions—in the level of other eye-stinging pollutants called oxidants.

*Cleaning tab.*    Then, of course, there is the thorniest problem of all: cost. "About 90% of pollutants can be removed simply," says Robert Russell, general manager of Koppers Co., Inc,'s Hardinge Co. "But 99% can double the cost." Senator Jackson estimates that the total tab for cleaning up the nation's pollution over the next five years at $15-billion for air, between $26-billion and $29-billion for our lakes and streams, and some $15-billion for solid-waste removal.

Industry spending is still only a fraction of that. But it is expanding steadily. According to a 1968 McGraw-Hill capital spending projection, industry forked out $1.5-billion that year for air and water pollution abatement—up 35% from 1967. Electric utilities have hiked their annual pollution-control spending to more than $300-million, steel companies are up to $325-million a year, and oil companies to more than $380-million a year. Humble Oil & Refining Co. alone raised its anti-pollution spending from $29-million in 1966 to more than $62-million in

1968. "To those who say they can't afford to take effective anti-pollution measures," says Humble Board Chairman M. A. Wright, "I can only respond that they can't afford not to." A. E. Joens, manager of environmental conservation in Humble's Western Production Division, has even put his off-shore crews under orders not to throw a single paper cup over the side. "There's only one way to keep air and water clean," Joens feels, "and that's not to pollute it."

*High cost of pollution.* The cost of pollution goes beyond tougher government regulation and an outraged citizenry. Incomplete combustion in factories and power plants now wastes some $300-million worth of sulfur each year. Once in the air, these and other pollutants corrode metal, weaken and fade fabrics and leathers, crack rubber, discolor paint, eat away concrete and building stone, and destroy $500-million worth of crops and livestock each year. The total annual tab for air pollution: $12-billion. For water pollution: several billion dollars more.

By tightening its water control measures, the pulp, paper, and paperboard industry annually recovers 1-million tons of reusable pulp fiber previously lost into rivers and lakes. American Can Co. converts its waste into a concentrate used for industrial adhesives and vanilla. Schenley Industries, Inc. is turning its distillery wastes into cattle feed. The Tennessee Valley Authority and U.S. Public Health Service are converting raw sewage and municipal waste into a soil conditioner. In 1968, San Francisco was even considering a proposal for changing garbage into electricity. This would involve building a $20-million incinerator that could burn up to 2,000 tons of garbage a day. The energy thus created would produce steam which, in turn, would produce electricity for Pacific Gas & Electric Co.

To cash in on what promises—someday—to be a huge market, almost everyone seems to be hitching a ride on the pollution control industry's express train. More than 1,000 companies now produce water control systems alone. With so much competition, many companies barely make ends meet. The question, says Louis Huff, product manager of water pollution control equipment for Robertshaw Controls Co., "is who can stand up the longest financially."

Some companies are standing up quite well. Research-Cottrell, Inc. has quadrupled its sales in five years (to $41-million). Over the last four years, Zurn Industries, Inc. has doubled its pollution control business (to $65-million), and raised it from 46% of the company's volume to 65%. Within the next five to seven years, Monsanto expects its budding air pollution control business to grow to more than $150-million, and the total air pollution market itself to go to $6-billion a year. Others project another $6-billion market for water pollution control.

## Beyond the City: New Parks and Entirely New Cities

As part of their antipollution offensive, some companies are trying to cope with another vexing environmental problem: inadequate park and recreation facilities. "In most of our city parks," Nixon's Citizens Advisory Committee on Environmental Quality warns, "maintenance is deplorable—worse than 30 years ago." The park problem is so deplorable, in fact, that the National Commission on Civil Disorders called it one of the major contributors to frustrations triggering ghetto riots. Take New York, where even 37,000 acres of parks, beaches, and playgrounds have long since proved unequal to modern population pressures. One recent park concert in Manhattan drew no fewer than 135,000 fans. Dozens of park sanitation men were three days clearing away the debris. "It's a nightmare," moans August Heckscher, New York City's parks commissioner.

Outside the city, 1-million acres of open space is lost every year to suburban development, new highways, industrial parks, airports, and other urban encroachments. Small wonder that a federal study group reported recently that in Yellowstone and several other national parks, "traffic congests the roads, frustrated fishermen struggle to find a place in line on the lakes." The U.S. Forest and National Park Services alone spend $4-million annually just to clean up after the 150-million people who visit national parks every year. Warns a recreation report published by Resources of the Future, Inc., a nonprofit corporation aided by the Ford Foundation: "We are approaching a grade-A crisis unprecedented in both size and character."

*Exceeding the minimum.* As heavy consumers of fresh water, hydroelectric utilities are required by law to set aside space for recreation. Many utilities, however, go beyond the minimum requirement. Since 1959, Pacific Gas & Electric Co. has poured $1-million into creating 58,000 acres of reservoirs, lakes, ponds, and other shoreline park areas on its 250,000 acres of California watershed land. Each year, more than 750,000 people tramp these areas. Philadelphia Electric Co, is focusing on a single park. As a dividend on the company's $70-million power plant located on the Susquehanna River, PE is spending $2.5-million to create the 500-acre Muddy Run Recreation Park. Among the park's conveniences: modern toilets and showers, coin-operated washers and dryers, charcoal grills, electrical outlets, camping sites for tents and trailers, and a boat dock and launching ramp on the park's 100-acre lake.

Outside of the government, one of the biggest public recreationists has to be International Paper Co. IP has opened up almost 90% of its 6.5-million acres of woodland to the public, and has created 40 parks with charcoal pits, fireplaces, weather shelters, swings, merry-go-rounds, and—where there are lakes—boat ramps. To help defray park maintenance costs, IP has also set aside some 150,000 acres in the South for fee hunting (squirrel, quail, an occasional turkey.)

At least one company, Olympia Brewing Co., hopes to turn a small profit on recreation. But recovering its full, initial investment may take years. On 260 acres of river bottomland outside Olympia, Wash., Olympia Brewing is spending $2.6–million on a recreational complex that will include an 18-hole championship golf course, two indoor swimming pools, four tennis courts, and a small lake. To build the park, Olympia literally had to move a mountain: it dug up almost 2-million cubic yards of dirt from a nearby hill and used it as fill. The company also took pains to guarantee that the golf course did not interfere with river fishing. "As a matter of fact," says Olympia Brewing President Robert A. Schmidt, "this will be the only course in the country where a sportsman will be able to get birdies and steelhead from the same area the same day." If all goes well, the entire park will be open in 1970, return its first profit in 1972, and move $40,000 to $50,000 in the black by 1975.

*Prepackaging.*    Some other companies are going outside the city and creating that far vaster urban complex—the "new town" or new city. They offer not only a model physical environment, but a prepackaged social and cultural environment as well.

Lovers of urban diversity continue to scorn such efforts. "It may be romantic," writes urbanologist Jane Jacobs, "to search for the salves of society's ills in slow-moving, rustic surroundings . . . but it is a waste of time. Does anyone suppose that . . . answers to any of the great questions that worry us today are going to come out of homogeneous settlements?"

Perhaps not. But new cities may be the only answer to today's population pressures, which certainly deepen and intensify society's ills. By the year 2000, the country's population will jump by 100-million people—half again as much as it is today. "That means that in this short span of time," Nixon told the 1969 National Governors Conference, "we will have to build the equivalent of 50 cities the size of Philadelphia." Or it means, as the National Committee on Urban Growth Policy recommends, that we should build 100 new cities averaging 100,000 in population, and 10 new cities averaging 1-million each.

*Profit and loss.*    Though new cities have taken root overseas—most notably in Finland and Britain—the American experience remains uneven. Gulf Oil Corp.'s Reston, Va., one of the most widely publicized of the new cities, ran into financial woes. A few miles outside of Phoenix, Goodyear Tire & Rubber Co.'s Litchfield Park is feeling the pinch of the tight mortgage market. Early in 1969, General Electric, which spent three years investigating 30 possible new-city sites, finally gave the whole thing up as unfeasible.

One standout success has been Humble Oil. Twenty miles south of Houston, Humble has created a sprawling complex consisting of Clear Lake City, a 15,434-acre community, and Bayport, a 7,250-acre industrial park. Though Humble made some early planning errors that still prick like prairie cactus, the overall project has been so successful that the company recently broke ground on another 50,000-acre community north of Houston, and a much smaller 245-acre community east of Houston.

Another notable success is Rouse Co.'s Columbia, Md. (see Chapter 6). Of the more than 100 new towns and cities that have sprung up across the country in the last several years, Columbia is among the few to be nearing profitability. Rouse Co.'s President James Rouse sees no reason why the country's problems of social and environmental blight would not yield to the same basic business principles that make a Columbia or a Clear Lake City successful. "Ours is the first nation in all history," Rouse notes, "that has the capacity to do whatever it has the will to do: replace men with computers, land men on the moon, eliminate poverty. Is it too much for such a nation to eliminate the ills which eat at its society?" Emphatically no, he answers. To do it, however, "we must equip ourselves with hope, with expectation, with demand for the best we know how to do, and that best must be much, much better than we are doing now." Businessmen, he feels, must move from being part of the problem to becoming part of the solution. "Urban growth is our opportunity," Rouse stresses, "not our enemy."

# 2

# William H. Wendel PRESIDENT, CARBORUNDUM CO.

*"The business of business is America"*

MEETING WILLIAM H. WENDEL is a little like seeing his neighboring Niagara Falls for the first time—rather more than you bargained for.

The recipient of *Business Week's* 1969 business citizenship award for "exceptional leadership," Wendel is president and chief executive officer of Carborundum Co., a $250-million company that produces everything from grinding wheels (300,000-odd models) to Spode china. He is president and founder of the Society for the Promotion, Unification, and Redevelopment of Niagara, Inc. (SPUR). He is chairman and one of the founders of the Local Governments Improvement Commission (LOGIC). He is one of nine commissioners serving on the Niagara Frontier Transportation Authority and a trustee of the Committee for Economic Development. He is also a man of fierce personal

41

commitment—and the awesome integrity of an umpire who is not afraid of getting beaned by an occasional bottle. "You can't involve yourself and not ruffle a few tempers," Wendel says. "Sometimes, that's the only way to get things done."

And when things need doing as urgently as they do today, Wendel feels, it is up to business—if only because business and society are products of the same complex and interrelated forces of change. Right now, of course, it is too early to tell whether today's social change and upheaval is good or bad. But to Wendel's thinking, there is no doubt that the parallel change in business is all to the good. "Pollution control," he says, "is no longer regarded as an unwarranted expense. It is an essential public objective. Urban renewal is not a socialistic encroachment, but the most effective means of rebuilding our cities. Training the disadvantaged is not an impossible task, but the only means of finding an adequate labor supply. Providing jobs is not a dole. It is a means of opening up vast new markets. Abandonment of certain employment testing is no longer a sacrifice of proper job placement. It is a recognition that test results and job performance may be unrelated. Plant investment in a ghetto is not an act of charity, so much as the quickest and best means to clean up the ghetto with little human anguish." And perhaps most important of all—"Providing leadership for a variety of quasi-public endeavors is not a detraction from corporate responsibilities, but a training and a broadening for higher corporate responsibilities."

Unfortunately, the same recognition and awareness has not dawned on all businessmen—at least not yet. But there are signs that it is coming. And so, too, is the recognition that, as Wendel puts it, "the corporation exists for society and not society for the corporation." Wendel views the modern corporation as a new tool of society. As such, it has the same motivation of profit and the same discipline of competition that it did before—with the added function of fulfilling man's social needs as it has already satisfied his material needs. "The business of business," Wendel says with conviction, "is America."

## A Few Seconds That Changed a City

In Wendel's home city of Niagara Falls, that particular business can be a full-time job. Despite its romantic honeymoon aura, the city has long had more troubles that the falls has tourists. These troubles began one hot afternoon in June, 1956. Less that two miles from the cascading waters that draw 4,500,000 tourists every year, an avalanche of rock thundered down the gorge of the Niagara River, crushing the Schoellkoph power station below it. In a few seconds, one of the world's cheapest sources of private power disappeared, and with it 25% of the city's tax base.

*Steady drain.* Over the next few years, the city's economy went into a long, slow fall. Old and established companies left the area or curtailed operations. Industrial employment tumbled from 35,000 to 20,000. The population slipped 10%, to 90,000. After five years of construction, the New York State Power Authority (SPA) completed an $800-million hydroelectric plant to replace the Schoellkoph station. The new plant, however, could not replace the tax base that the Schoellkoph station had provided. So when 95% of the SPA work force left Niagara Falls and took their purchasing power with them, "the impact was like a meat cleaver behind the ears," notes Mayor E. Dent Lackey, a former Carborundum executive.

Wendel further roiled the waters, after he moved up from Carborundum's assistant to the president to president in 1962. In a wrenching reorganization, Wendel slashed costs, redesigned the company into tight profit centers, appointed new young group vice presidents to supervise these centers, embarked on an ambitious acquisition and diversification program, and—to the consternation of the city fathers—fired more than 300 high-priced, middle-management executives. "The politicians and chamber of commerce paraded to my door," Wendel recalls, "and we had some long meetings." Wendel was the first to admit that the city was in deep trouble. "The spark had gone out of our urban life," he says. "The city was on the skids." Everyone agreed that Niagara Falls needed new leadership, "and I felt I should provide it," Wendel notes, "since we're the only large national company with headquarters here."

*Some pointers.*    Going on the road, Wendel personally elicited support from every business leader whose company had facilities in Niagara Falls. He also travelled to Pittsburgh for a first-hand look at the accomplishments—and lessons—of that city's Allegheny Conference, the organization formed by Pittsburgh's business establishment in 1943 to combat pollution, ugly commercial slums, and other urban blight.

In Pittsburgh, conference members passed along some valuable advice. "They recommended that we form an entirely new citizens' organization," says Wendel, "and stay clear of existing organizations like the chamber of commerce. That way, you can design a whole new framework for problem-solving, and not be stigmatized by what these other community groups have tried and failed to do in the past." Wendel was also warned against membership drives with a broad scope. "Get financing, they told me, from a limited number of organizations, and let your membership be one thing and your financial support another." An added piece of advice for promoting community cooperation: "Stay out of the limelight and let the other fellow get the credit—and publicity. Nothing promotes cooperation like the promise of public recognition."

*Community catalyst.*    What finally emerged was SPUR, a private, nonprofit citizens group that, as Wendel described it, "would serve as a catalyst for community action, and operate for three to five years—depending on how long it took us to catalyze the community." SPUR was not intended as an action organization. That is, it would not carry out urban redevelopment, for example. More than that, says Wendel, "it would try to identify problems, mobilize resources—particularly human resources—and help organize and coordinate these people and other resources to solve our city's most pressing problems." To help sell the idea, Wendel invited 50 local civic and business leaders to his office for cocktails, "and from the first made it clear that this would not be a very democratic organization. I simply insisted on being the permanent president. I wanted to be sure I was not starting something I wouldn't be able to finish. This," he adds with a wry grin, "was to make our annual election of officers a bit of a joke."

Business quickly rallied to his banner. Forty-one of the city's largest industrial, commercial, and banking firms pledged $42,000 to cover SPUR's first-year operating expenses. At the same time, 66 leading citizens from business, labor, education, the news media, and cultural groups signed on as charter members, volunteering whatever time they could spare. Of the ten members that Wendel asked to serve on SPUR's board of directors, not one refused. Among them were top local executives from Hooker Chemical Corp., Kimberly Clark Corp., Union Carbide, and Du Pont, as well as Paul A. Schoellkoph, Jr., president of Schoell-Penn Corp. and one of the city's wealthiest and most influential businessmen.

## High Hopes and Hard Realities

Amid high hopes and expectations, SPUR opened for business in October, 1964. Almost immediately, it ran into some hard realities—namely, citizen apathy and local government distrust. As one of its first campaigns, SPUR plumped for a proposed city charter revision—and lost. It sought a community college for Niagara Falls—and lost. It sought a proposed Atomic Energy Commission laboratory—and lost. It tried to get the city to appoint a professional city manager, rather than a politician. SPUR lost that one, too. From the first, Mayor Lackey's government felt instinctively suspicious of this upstart citizens' group, and "relations grew worse," says one SPUR board member, "before they got better. That first year saw some pretty angry shouting matches."

SPUR also had internal problems. Executive director Robert A. Cox, Jr., a civil engineer and planner with wide background in public and private community development, showed a keen ability for organizing and planning. But when it came to executing his plans, says one SPUR member, "he generated more paper than results." About the time Wendel and other board members were becoming disillusioned with Cox, he joined Mayor Lackey's government as head of the city's Urban Renewal Agency—only to be fired eight months later for stepping on too many political toes.

With Cox's departure from SPUR, Wendel began casting around for a replacement. "That first appointment had been a mistake," Wendel admits. "We insisted on a professional when we should have picked someone more familiar and more concerned with the community and its people." Until a permanent director could be found, Wendel and the rest of SPUR's board decided to turn the job over to one of their own members, Mrs. John Runals, a shrewd, articulate, and astute attorney, and—by her own admission—"a rank amateur" in urban development. Mrs. Runals soon proved so effective that she became the permanent director. "If anyone had asked me at first to do the job permanently," she claims, "I would have said 'absolutely, not.' But one comes to see the value of the amateur's approach. You don't know what you can't do, therefore almost anything becomes possible or at least worth a try."

*Change of heart.* By the time Mrs. Runals took over, SPUR's relations with local government were shaping up, and SPUR and Mayor Lackey's administration were beginning to coordinate their efforts toward one single objective: improvement of the city's environment to keep industry from moving out and, perhaps more importantly, to keep the tourists pouring in. "It is going to be tourism supporting this city now, not industry," Wendel feels. "Our goal then, is to lure more tourists, and to keep them for greater lengths of time."

Such an attitude marked an abrupt departure for the city. In the late 1950s when the Schoellkoph power station was destroyed, tourists were merely tolerated as a profitable nuisance. The city showed it—and still does. Ringing the clean but unimpressive state park on the American side of Niagara Falls is a dismal downtown of squat two- and three-story buildings, honkytonk souvenir shops, and rundown hotels. But once across the Rainbow Bridge connecting Niagara Falls, N.Y. and Niagara Falls, Ontario, tourists find themselves in an idyllic setting of shrubbed and manicured gardens, tasteful little gift shops, good restaurants, and two large hotels overlooking the falls. "We began to realize," notes Hamilton B. Mizer, publisher of the Niagara Falls Gazette and a member of SPUR's board, "that tourists were spending two or three hours on the American side, then crossing to the Canadian falls where they would spend the night and their money."

To help hold onto the tourists, the city commissioned a land development study by Candeub, Flessig & Associates, the large Newark-based planning firm. When the study was completed, Wendel asked Gregory Mandeville, Carborundum's director for Latin America and the Pacific, to head a five-man SPUR task force and review the plan. "We held eight meetings, studied the whole plan, and found it very disappointing," says Mandeville. "Basically, it accepted the status quo and did not provide for new or improved land usage. It retained the old strip development type of shopping. There was no provision for social needs. It ignored education completely. It presumed that larger merchants and downtown retailers wanted to be in the tourist area, which was just not true. And it spotted one department store on one end of the downtown, another on the other end, and a third in the center. This ignored the basic need for competitive shopping and the fact that Macy's and Gimbel's for instance, like to be next door to each other."

*Baying at the moon.* Mandeville reported his task force findings back to Wendel. They both agreed that a negative report by SPUR would accomplish nothing, since SPUR had no political leverage. "Bill and I decided," says Mandeville, "that what we should do was set up a permanent committee to work on a comprehensive development plan that would use the Candeub, Flessig plan as a starting point and something to build on." SPUR then organized a meeting, with Mandeville as chairman, and invited downtown merchants and city planners. "We were sort of the dogs baying at the moon," says Mandeville. "We presented the Candeub, Flessig plan without comment and simply asked the merchants their opinion." Sure enough, the merchants said they did not want to be in the tourist section. At that time, in fact, many of them were moving to the suburbs because of high taxes. "The city planners heard all this," says Mandeville, "and saw that the merchants were just not supporting the plan."

Out of the meeting, local merchants got together with SPUR, formed a Commercial Core Committee, and hired Alexander & Moskowitz, Inc., a New York planning firm, to make another land usage study. Picking up where the merchants left off, A&M advocated a tourist district directly adjacent to the state park and the falls, and a separate redeveloped commercial core overlapping the tourist district just enough to promote some intermingling. Other smaller merchants who wanted to be in the tourist section organized the Rainbow Center Committee, and began similar planning. Eventually, both committees came together, and formed the Niagara Falls Gateway to America Corp., an independent, nonprofit development organization. Composed of representatives from 23 major companies and capitalized—

through company and individual pledges—at $75,000 a year, Gateway hoped to work with the city government and help coordinate a master downtown development plan. As Gateway envisioned its role, it would sell other outside developers on investing in Niagara Falls and in assuming the financial burden for revitalizing the downtown.

## Awakening a New Vitality and Spirit

To get things moving, Gateway officials began talking with urban renewal experts all over the country, including government officials in Washington. The corporation, however, overlooked one key area: local government sensibilities. Almost immediately, the city fathers were up in arms again. "Quite logically," says John Runals, Gateway's vice president and secretary, "they felt their sacred cow had been gored. They felt we were attacking their urban renewal program and impugning their reputations." At one stage, adds Gateway President Kenneth Rickert, "things reached a point where the city demanded to know just whom we were fronting for. They regarded us as a threat to them, and felt we were going behind their backs."

Finally, R. Wolcott Hooker, Gateway's board chairman, went to the city's Urban Renewal Agency and had it out. "I am frankly surprised," he told the mayor and other agency officials, "that you should expect me to ask you to hold my hand as I pass through doors freely opened to me as a result of my long years of recognized integrity and perhaps some expertise in the field of industry and public service." Hooker assured the agency and city government that neither he nor Gateway had any "ulterior motive." He was not asking Gateway's board "to finance an excursion up a blind alley. I do not choose to engage in a game of cops and robbers. There is nothing in my motives or those of my fellow board members which does not meet the eye." Gateway sought only to establish a close working relationship with the city, he said, and to be designated by the city as the preferred redeveloper of the downtown area. Hooker's remarks struck home. Unofficially, Gateway is now the preferred redeveloper, and the corporation's relations with the city "are as warm," says Rickert, "as they could be expected to be."

*On the way.*    Today, most of the city's 80-acre downtown has been earmarked for urban renewal, and some $23-million in federal, state, and city funds has been pledged to the project. Toward the end of 1969, land was being bulldozed for a $17-million convention hall, designed by architect Philip Johnson. Slopping around the convention hall's muddy construction site, Mayor Lackey brimmed with pride and enthusiasm. "This building will cover 25 acres when completed in 1972," he said. "It will be built under a huge rainbow-shaped arch nine stories high at its highest point. It will seat 8,900 people, have a 500-seat enclosed amphitheater, 8,000 sq. ft. of exhibit storage area, offices, television facilities, several conference and meeting rooms, including one with 2,000 seats—everything. What this convention hall has come to represent—a new metropolitan vitality, spirit, awareness—our city government could never have brought off alone. Neither could Bill Wendel. But together we are doing it." Immediately adjacent to the convention hall site, Carborundum is planning a $20-million complex. It will include a new company headquarters building, a bank, a museum to house a ceramic display of Carborundum's Spode chine, and several fancy plazas.

"When both the convention hall and Carborundum project become a working reality," predicts Gateway's Rickert, "we will be able to generate real interest and excitement among developers, and this whole program should take off." That is, once the money market loosens up. "Right now," Gateway's John Runals notes, "it's very tight, and we feel it in our conversations with developers. Many of them are already over-extended." But Rickert and Runals—along with almost everyone else within Gateway and SPUR—are confident that the developers will come around eventually. To hear Wendel talk, in fact, it is almost as inevitable as the 760,000 gal. of water that go crashing over the falls every second. "One has only to look around," Wendel says. "With a little planning and hard work on the community's part, how could this area miss?"

How, indeed. Beyond the commercial attraction of the falls and the economic lure of cheap, plentiful power, the city lies in the center of the rich Northeast market. It is within one day's trucking and rail freight distance of 63% of the 165,000 industrial firms located in the country's top 100 industrial market counties. Within a radius of 500 miles, there is a consumer market of more than 100-million people. Within the smaller Niagara Frontier—the area encompassing Niagara and Erie Counties and comprising the 14th largest metropolitan area in the country—are more than 1,350,000 people.

## Realignment toward Social Involvement

In today's complex and troubled times, however, it takes more than a commercial environment for a community to succeed. It also takes the proper social climate, and SPUR is also trying to elevate that aspect of the local life.

SPUR's social involvement is part of a broad realignment that grew out of a policy study which SPUR commissioned from Murray V. Jones & Associates Ltd., of Toronto. The study made three major recommendations. It suggested that SPUR: (1) do more long-range policy planning and less "fire-fighting," (2) expand its scope beyond the city to include all of Niagara County and possibly beyond, and (3) stop considering itself a short-term organization. "It was a mistake," says Wendel, "to start out thinking that within three to five years we could generate all the programs that needed generating. But then again, who could have anticipated all the social change that was to come, and that

SPUR itself would have to plunge into so many social areas to help solve some of the area's economic problems. We also discovered that we weren't dealing with problems, so much as change. And we had to change with the community and the times."

Housing was one major social problem. Niagara Falls is a city of old homes—many of them in low-income areas and in desperate need of renovation. To help alleviate the condition—and promote a little local ecumenicism—SPUR brought together the area's 16 churches and synagogues and organized the Interfaith Housing Corp. SPUR also spurred formation of the Niagara Frontier Housing Development Corp. This is a nonprofit development group created to take advantage of low-cost federal programs and to promote new and rehabilitated housing in both Niagara and neighboring Erie Counties. Toward the end of 1969, the two corporations were rehabilitating 500 housing units, building 460 new units, and had plans for another 2,000 or so units in 1970.

*Demand for new perspectives.*    On a broader social level, SPUR also created an Urban Coalition—highly unusual in a city the size of Niagara Falls. Even more unusual was Wendel's successful effort to merge the coalition with the local United Givers Fund and Council of Social Agencies. Over the previous 10 or 15 years, there had been half a dozen efforts to bring UGF and Council of Social Agencies together. "But they went nowhere," says John Claydon, senior vice president of Carborundum and UGF president at the time of the merger. "This was because of the usual rivalries, jealousies, and the one big question as to which of the two would be the surviving or dominant organization."

Four months after organizing the Urban Coalition, Wendel decided to make another try at merger—this time on a three-way basis. He talked with leaders of the Urban Coalition, then fired off a challenging letter to the boards of UGF and Council of

Social Agencies. "The policies, programs, and organizations of the United Givers Fund, Council of Social Agencies, and their member agencies have not kept pace with the urban crisis," he wrote. "No social upheaval has been so far-reaching and significant. Our cities will never be the same again. These dramatic, momentous forces demand changes in the entire structure of organizations serving the needs of health and social welfare."

Wendel noted that in years past UGF had been the prime, if not sole, group dealing with social problems. "Today," he wrote, "more and more local, state, and federal governments participate, direct, and supply funds." In the same way, the Council of Social Agencies had for years been the prime, if not sole, planner of local social programs. Now, Wendel observed, all governmental units maintain planning departments. "A merging of public activities in health and social welfare with private activities in these areas will become increasingly important," he stressed. "The staggering cost of carrying out the necessary programs demands this amalgamation." Wendel proposed that the city's three major social agencies pool their resources and form an entirely new group with new structure, new objectives, and new outlook. The consolidated organization—to be called the Niagara Coalition—would focus on "jobs, housing, education, training, recreation, and individual concern for the less fortunate, together with a continuation of the most essential existing programs."

*Resurgence of a rivalry.* Wendel followed his letter up with telegrams to 31 key officials of local government and the three agencies, proposing a merger meeting, "I'll never forget that meeting," he recalls. "The invitations went out only a few days beforehand, and it was held on Sunday of the July 4 weekend in 1968. Despite our bad timing, 27 people showed up." And all of them supported Wendel's idea. They chose a committee to work out the details, elected Carborundum's John Claydon as temporary committee chairman, and scheduled the first committee meeting for the next day. "Then some of the old jealousies flared up again," recalls one committee member. "Claydon had been president of the United Givers Fund. So some of the boys from the Council of Social Agencies got together, and when Claydon convened the first committee meeting, they pushed through a motion installing the past president of the council as temporary chairman." Claydon ran the meeting for all of five minutes, "and I can tell you his head was spinning."

Everything worked out in the end, however. Today, the Niagara Coalition is a functioning, going concern. As might be expected, it has its problems blending personalities and programs into an organic whole. But the fact that it merely exists is a rare triumph. And Owen Mahony, Niagara Coalition's executive director, firmly feels that his combined organization will succeed where many local Urban Coalitions are bound to fail. "They are dying," he feels, "because they are not really coalitions in the sense that we are. You must attack today's social problems not in terms of race, as the Urban Coalition does. That only sharpens racial polarities. You must attack these problems in terms of people, black and white. Our problems today go much deeper than race. And you must have the full, dedicated concern of local community leaders. We certainly have that in Bill Wendel."

Mahony recalls first meeting Wendel back in the early 1960s. "At first," Mahony says, "he struck me as the stereotyped corporate giant—a man with very little sensitivity, one who knew how to throw his weight around but was so sure of himself that he didn't even bother." Mahony admits he was "100% wrong." Wendel, he feels, "was just keeping his distance from people, and he still does that to some degree. But Bill started giving himself away in the men he gathered around him at Carborundum—deeply committed people like Gregory Mandeville and John Claydon." Several months before the Urban Coalition came into being, Mahony attended a meeting at Wendel's home, and the conversation turned to inner-city problems. "We got to talking," says Mahony, "about rats, chronic unemployment, the hopelessness and despair you run into with minority groups—and suddenly I noticed that Bill was actually on the verge of tears. He was not just concerned, but deeply and genuinely anxious about these people—to the point of being overpowered by his emotions. For me, this was a terribly moving experience."

## Down to Fundamentals: the Maze of Metropolitan Government

At the same time that Wendel was creating the Urban Coalition and merging it into the broader Niagara Coalition, his mind was turning toward an even more fundamental problem—one that nearly all metropolitan areas share today—that is, inefficient local government. "You can have the brightest and best citizen community group in the country," says Wendel. "But unless you have a government structure geared to work with and for the community, you can end up just spinning your wheels."

To improve local traction, SPUR formed a partnership with the New York State Joint Legislative Committee on Metropolitan and Regional Areas Study, and organized the Local Governments Improvement Commission (LOGIC). Its purpose: to make a study of the 21 county, city, town, and village governments of Niagara County and offer recommendations for more effective administration. "We are not looking at people in government and how they individually do their jobs," says Wendel, who serves as LOGIC's chairman. "We are looking at functions of government, at total structure, and the role that local government should play in these very complex times we live in."

*High toll.* Forming five task forces of 10 to 12 citizens each, LOGIC spent eight months combing through the maze of local government, interviewed nearly 90 public officials, and documented the usual case of widespread and wasteful duplication: 17 separate tax rolls prepared by 31 assessors, 20 separate unco-

ordinated development plans, 21 highway departments, 21 pyr-
amiding tax and debt limits, seven different levels of police protection, 15 sewer systems, 28 water systems. A typical householder
in Niagara Falls pays $3.96 every three months for water. A
resident in nearby Wilson pays $16.20 for the same amount of
water. The town of Hartland spent $749.19 per lane-mile of
highway in 1969. The town of Niagara spent $2,186.49 per lane-
mile. Partly as a result of such imbalance and inefficiency and
partly because of inflation, the total annual budget of the county's 21 local governments has spiralled 120% since 1960 (to $73-
million)—during a period when the county's population was declin-
ing 3%. "Perhaps the best case for change," says SPUR's Mrs.
Runals, who doubles as executive director of LOGIC, "came out
of our own difficulty in just getting information. No one was
hiding anything. They just couldn't always come up with answers. In some cases, local officials didn't even know how many
employees they had."

Toward the end of 1969, LOGIC wound up its study. The
final report laid out all the problems and recommended creation
of a single, county-wide government consisting of an elected
Community Executive and a Community Council with representatives from every election district and several members at large.
Niagara County has a valuable precedent in Florida, where Du-
val County and the city of Jacksonville were consolidated into a
single metropolitan unit in 1968. "We're going way beyond
that," says William Branche, assistant director of LOGIC. "Florida joined two governments. We want to join 21." Before sharing LOGIC's final report with the public, Wendel presided at a
special meeting of the county's mayors, supervisors, and other
assorted public officials who heard it. "Most of them," says Mrs.
Runals, "came prepared to find fault, and none of them gave a
damn about who Wendel was or what he was trying to do. They
didn't owe him a thing. But Bill really won them over. He is not
a good public speaker, in the textbook sense. But he does estab-

lish a rare rapport with an audience. And he listens closely when someone else has the floor." When it was all over, the politicians gave Wendel a warm applause, and a vote of confidence on the direction that LOGIC was moving. After a series of public hearings that will run into early 1970, LOGIC's recommendations will go to a public referendum—"that is," says Wendel, "if initial response at our hearings is favorable. We want to be sure we have public support on this."

*Crisp sequence.*   In his dealings within LOGIC and SPUR, Wendel runs things the way he runs his business—with crisp military authority and precision. It comes naturally. A graduate of the U. S. Naval Academy, Wendel spent seven years in the Navy, joined Carborundum in 1947 as assistant to the president, and moved up to the top spot in 1962. He won a quick reputation—both at Carborundum and in civic affairs—as a man who relished broader, long-range strategy more than tight, narrow control. "American industry," he likes to say, "is turning more and more to management by objectives, to the qualification of targets." Setting those targets, Wendel feels, may be even more challenging than actually reaching them. "You can go almost anywhere," he says, "as long as you go in the right sequence."

And what is the right sequence for SPUR? Where does it go from here? Wendel shrugs aside such questions. "We may move into a pollution abatement campaign," he says with a wink toward his office window and some of Carborundum's belching stacks outside. "It's hard to say. We still consider our current work unfinished. Our involvement is completely open-ended, as it has to be when you're attacking problems like these." Wendel is also quick to admonish against calling SPUR a "success," or holding it out as the answer to the urban crisis. "Every city is different," he stresses. "With only 90,000 people in Niagara Falls and 234,000 in the county, we are small enough here that our situation is workable. This is very important. I don't see how anyone could ever solve the problems, for instance, in New York

City. Certainly, we haven't solved the problems of Niagara Falls. We have made mistakes. But we have also made a start, and that's what is important."

In a recent speech to some businessmen, Wendel discussed his company's acquisition program and raised—as well as answered—some pertinent questions. "The chances of complete success?" he asked. "Nil. Have we lost people? Yes. Will we in the future? Yes. Is the game worth the candle? Definitely, yes." Wendel could almost have been describing his own personal experience and expectations in the revitalization of Niagara Falls.

# 3

## Levi Strauss & Co.

*"We wanted to go beyond tokenism"*

WALTER HAAS, JR., PRESIDENT of Levi Strauss & Co., always gets a little miffed when someone singles his company out for its good works in the ghetto. "We are doing much," he admits, "and we can and will do more. But instead of being the good example, we would much rather be only one of an overwhelming majority doing what should and must be done." Yet an example his company remains. After the 1967 Detroit riots and the formation of the National Alliance of Businessmen, President Johnson appointed Haas as one of eight regional chairmen to help head up the NAB's nationwide ghetto job program. In 1969, a Harvard alumni group named Haas "business statesman of the year." And six months later, Levi Strauss & Co. received one of two 1969 *Business Week* citizenship awards for its efforts in "human resources."

59

In Haas, the drive for corporate profits and a concern for disadvantaged minorities pulse like an alternating current. You cannot really separate the two, he feels, and still hope to survive in today's torturous and swiftly changing times. The disadvantaged, Haas says, "are not just temporary victims of an economic cycle, as some people claim. They are permanently poor, without jobs, and worst of all without hope. Some people shrug and say, 'Let them pull themselves up.' But how are you going to lift yourself by your bootstraps if you don't have any bootstraps?" The civil rights progress of the last 15 years, he adds, "hasn't even touched the hardcore unemployed in the ghettos. In fact, they're being left further and further behind. Too many fine-sounding programs, announced with much fanfare, have failed. Too many promises have been broken. Too many hopes have been left unfulfilled. So people are alienated, anguished—and angry—and feel that nobody cares. Is it any wonder they can be easily moved to violence?"

Haas quotes some figures put together by one of his fellow NAB chairmen, Clyde Skeen, president of Ling-Temco-Vought, Inc. They show that the average productive person taken off the welfare rolls and placed in a steady job will:

- Contribute $10,000 per year to the gross national product.
- Pay federal and state income taxes of $300 a year.
- Increase purchasing power for goods and services by $3,400 a year.
- Relieve the government of welfare or support payments of $1,308 a year.
- Cut unemployment costs and the need for welfare and other community services.

In Haas' own NAB region, which covers five Western states, Haas cites another study by Sacramento's City Planning Commission. The commission explored the city's substandard housing areas, where most of the unemployed live, and found that they represented 20% of the population, but paid only 12% of the taxes. They accounted for 42% of adult crime, 36% of the juvenile delinquency, and 26% of the fires. They also represented 76% of reported cases of tuberculosis, consumed 50% of the city's health services, 41% of the police protection, and 25% of the fire protection. "I'd call that pretty strong incentive for business to do something," says Haas. "The simple fact of the matter is that government has failed. That's why it has called on business. Six out of every seven jobs in the nation are in the private sector. It must be done by business if it's going to be done at all."

Will business do it? Haas is hopeful—but cautiously so. "Two things frighten me terribly," he admits. "One is the large number of supposedly responsible business leaders who apparently still do not see the necessity for adjusting their traditional attitudes to conform to the realities of the modern world. The problems are not passive. They are not simply going to disappear. They are going to grow and compound at a terrifying rate unless we solve them." Equally alarming, Haas feels, is the "attitude of those who, while seeing the tide approaching, try to stem it through nothing more than lip service. This is a sort of hypocritical appeasement which does nothing but build false hopes and ultimately leads to the destruction of whatever faith remains in the business institution's willingness to face facts."

## A History of Minority Hiring

Levi Strauss & Co. has been facing the social facts for a good many years now. The venerable, 119-year-old company, which produces $230-million worth of its popular blue-denim "Levi's" a year, received much of its minority impetus from Haas himself. As the young personnel manager of the privately-owned company which his great grand-uncle founded, Haas hired the company's first Negro employee back in 1946. He was Booker T. Washington, who still works for the company in its San Francisco headquarters. Two years later, Haas also hired the company's first Negro woman for a summer job as a data processing clerk. "We got the predictable complaints," Haas recalls. "Some of the other women, for instance, did not want to share the same restroom with her. I said, 'Fine, then go to the other building and use that one.'" By the end of the summer, a permanent job opened up and Haas talked again with the women. "The change in their attitude was about what I expected," he says. "They agreed that she should get the job, and she did."

*Storm signals.* The company took the same approach in 1962 when it decided—against towering odds—to integrate its manufacturing and distribution plants in the South. "We wanted to go beyond tokenism," says Haas. "So we decided to use the economic leverage of our payroll." The idea itself originated with Paul Glasgow, vice president of operations. "Back in those days," Glasgow recalls, "there were no real ghetto troubles as we know them today. But there was a lot of ghetto grumbling, and people were becoming more and more conscious that something was wrong."

Glasgow himself recalls his own early concerns, and waking up late one night, "wondering 'what am I doing for these people?' The answer was 'nothing,' and I decided then and there it was time we made an effort." The next morning, Glasgow went to Walter and Peter Haas—the latter, Walter's brother and the company's executive vice president. "Up to then," Peter Haas recalls, "we had tolerated segregation in our Southern plants with the feeling that—well, was it really up to us to try to change and dictate the mores of the South? We knew segregation was wrong. But I suppose we lacked the courage of our convictions. When Paul came in and we all started talking, we saw what we had to do, and that we would simply have to go ahead and take the consequences."

*Definition.* In integrating that first plant in 1962, the company contacted the local chamber of commerce, businessmen, the churches, politicians. Recalls Peter Haas: "Their first question was, okay, what kind of integration? If it had to come, they suggested putting the blacks on one side of the plant, the whites on the other, and separating the two with a partition. When we said no to that, they suggested a line down the middle of the plant." The company said no again, and insisted on total integration. "Needless to say," Glasgow notes, "we didn't get one bit of help from the white community." So the company appealed directly to its white workers in the city. "We talked to every employee in groups of ten," says Glasgow. "We told them we didn't have to integrate, but that we felt a social and moral responsibility, and that we were going to do it." The company had $1.5-million invested in the plant, and stood to lose it all. At one point, Peter Haas asked Glasgow how the odds stood. "I told him 50–50," Glasgow says. "He then asked what we'd do if we lost there, and I told him we should move on to the next plant and try to integrate that one."

Most of the community and the apparel industry alike expected the company to lose. "But in the end," Glasgow beams happily, "we lost only one girl. And she said she agreed with us but that her husband was making her quit." From that plant, Levi Strauss went on to integrate its other Southern facilities—now numbering 30. As a follow-up, the company also notified its suppliers and contract plants that they were expected to integrate, as well.

*Fresh view.* After his appointment as an NAB chairman, Haas took a new look at his company's minority hiring, and decided Levi Strauss was still not doing enough. As part of its NAB commitment, the company pledged to hire at least 5% of its new employees from among the hardcore unemployed, and set up training programs that raised their retention rate to 70%—comparable to that of regular employees. "And by hardcore," says Glasgow, "I mean hard hardcore. I want those real tough ones that have little or no work experience—those people that no one else will hire. These are the ones who really need a break."

In its San Francisco headquarters, the company created a special stenographers pool just for minority trainees. They receive $75 a week to start, train an average of four months, then move into higher paying clerical and secretarial jobs. One of these trainees came to the company typing 17 words per minute. Today, she is up to 60 wpm. In one of its Southern plants, Levi Strauss even hired a Negro woman who had served time for armed robbery. "Sure, we had our problems with her," Glasgow admits. "She had those usual Monday morning blues, and often required a special escort to work. And despite the fact that our local people told her about the pill, she soon got pregnant with a second illegitimate child." But during the time she worked for the company, the woman received two merit pay increases. "So we are keeping her job open," says Glasgow, "and when she has her baby she will have a place with us if she wants to come back."

As part of the company's new hiring policy, says Theodore Freeman, a bright young Negro in the corporate personnel department, "we try to screen people in rather than screen them out." When high school dropout Robert Mitchell applied for a job, for instance, his only work experience had been in canneries and other menial jobs, and he had been unemployed for seven months. To test Mitchell's aptitude, the company gave him a special abstract test that ignored the word and math questions that normally confuse disadvantaged youngsters. It showed that Mitchell had an above-average aptitude for computer work. One year after joining the company, he is now in a challenging spot as a junior computer programmer.

*Management opening.*    Levi Strauss is also going beyond entry-level jobs for the disadvantaged. Over the last few years, it has begun upgrading minority employees. Today, 14% of the company's 1,000 supervisory and managerial employees come from minority groups. Among them is one man who has two convictions for armed robbery. "These are not top-level positions, at least not yet," Haas stresses. "But they are positions in supervision and management, and they can be steps up the ladder." Barbara Clemens, a Negro who joined Levi Strauss in 1958 as a mail clerk, is now one of three product managers in the Levi's for Gals Div. As a member of middle-management, she is responsible for coordinating and supervising production, sales, and final distribution of a complete product line. "One comes to accept opportunities like this in the home office," she says. "But sometime in 1970, I'll be making my first business trip to Alabama, and I don't know how much they'll accept it down there. It should be interesting."

## Peaks and Valleys of Minority Ownership

Along with minority employees, Levi Strauss is trying to create minority employers, as well. As a starter, Haas offered to provide opening expenses and working capital for a menswear store in San Francisco's Hunters Point-Bayview district, the scene of a violent 1966 riot. What Haas proposed—and a local black community group accepted—was that the group assume ownership of the store and designate three young trainees to study management and sales with Levi Strauss and other cooperating retailers. "Everything sounded fine in theory," says Haas. "But we ran into one problem after another." The blacks grew impatient with the training, and Levi Strauss grew impatient with their impatience. Finally, the whole deal seemed to fall through. "We had a long session one day, and were getting nowhere," recalls Haas. "So I said, 'Look, let's break this off for now. Any time you are willing to talk and want to see me, I'll make myself available.' Six weeks later—with no warning, not even a phone call—half a dozen of them burst into my office during an important meeting. 'Here we are,' they said, 'We want to talk.' They were not being funny or sarcastic. They just had no concept of procedure or the fact that I had a business to run."

*Wrong track.* About the same time, Levi Strauss was combing the black community for a retail administrator to coordinate its minority store ownership program. More than 200 applicants had been screened down to seven when an affable, articulate young Negro named Lonnie Poindexter contacted Freeman and Mel Bacharach, vice president of marketing. Poindexter was not looking for a job. After 6½ years at Al's Men's Shop in the Oakland ghetto, Poindexter was making $10,000 a year as store manager and was helping run a $350,000-a-year business that he hoped to own one day. "I had heard what Levi Strauss was trying to do," he says, "and I just thought I'd see if I could offer some ideas." After talking with Freeman and Bacharach, Poindexter was ushered in to see Haas himself. "It was the first time I'd ever met a white businessman so eager and so emotionally anxious to help," Poindexter recalls. "But he didn't have any concept of how to promote minority ownership. What he was saying and doing just didn't make sense." Poindexter made plenty of sense to Haas, however, and Haas persuaded him to join the company as retail administrator.

As one of his first assignments, Poindexter entered the sticky negotiations over the Hunters Point-Bayview store. "Our black community group thought this was a fine idea," Haas notes. "But Lonnie was what they politely termed a 'house nigger,' and they said he had to have a 'shadow,' hired from the community group. This was to be Lonnie's right-hand man and would go wherever Lonnie went. The shadow's job was to give Lonnie credibility in the black community." To keep the store idea alive, Haas agreed to a shadow, expecting to pay $2 or so an hour. "But the man they picked," Haas marvels, "said, 'Oh no, I'm an executive. I'm going to be Lonnie's top assistant.' We ended up paying him $600 or $700 a month." Despite Poindexter's best efforts, the idea for the store—along with Poindexter's ubiquitous shadow—quietly faded away.

*Blank check.* Because of the tangle of problems involved, Poindexter has guided Levi Strauss away from any further such involvement. "You don't help the minority businessman by handing him everything on a platter," Poindexter feels. "What he needs is training, advice, help in getting loans, and a feeling that the white man really cares." Poindexter cites the case of a friend who lives in the East Palo Alto ghetto. "Just across the tracks in Atherton, Calif.," he says, "there was this group of white liberals and do-gooders who got together and decided to help the black man. They asked my friend and some other blacks what they could do. 'We want to control our businesses,' my friend told them. 'Fine,' they said. 'What businesses can you run?' Just out of the air, my friend suggested a clothing store. A week later he got a call from a local branch bank manager. 'I've got a cashier's check here for you for $25,000,' the manager said. In other words, do your thing, baby. Now, man, who gets a blank check for $25,000—with no collateral, no assets, no experience?" His friend's backers obviously did not consider this an investment. It was charity. "Otherwise," says Poindexter, "they would have followed up to see that my friend was properly trained, that he had the right inventory, the right store location, that he hired the right people. When you invest money, you sure as hell want to know where every nickel goes. But they didn't give a damn. So why should he?" Within a year, the store was going under and his creditors were bringing suit.

Even for blacks who know the business, the problems are monumental. Witness Sarah Johnson and Ella Oden. They are two pert, young married sisters who went to business school and decided to open a women's high-fashion boutique in downtown Pittsburg, Calif. Levi Strauss helped arrange their SBA and bank contacts, and 30 weeks of training in a Berkeley women's store. "Our sales people," says Jean Harris, owner of the Berkeley store, "passed on everything they knew. I also took the girls on my buying trips and all the sales representatives with whom we came in contact gave us their wholehearted support and interest." After getting assurance of an SBA guarantee, the two sisters went to four banks—and were turned down by all four. Among the banks was the local branch of Bank of America, a member of the $2-million "Opportunity through Ownership" consortium set up just to finance minority businesses. Bank of America is also a bank on which Walter Haas, Jr. sits as a board member. "Even with his high position," says Mrs. Johnson, "Mr. Haas was more than two weeks on the telephone before he could get our loan approved." When Bank of America finally came through with $14,400, SBA suddenly held up its guarantee. "By then," sighs Mrs. Oden, "we were going around in circles." Poindexter helped arrange another meeting with SBA and bank representatives, and SBA finally guaranteed the bank loan. The Sisters Boutique is now grossing more than $4,000 a month, which is above earlier projections. But it still has troubles. "For some reason," says Mrs. Oden, "we're not getting the black business. They buy in white stores, but not in ours."

Or consider Hury Thornton. With counseling from Levi Strauss, Thornton set up Breed Men's Shop in San Francisco's East Oakland ghetto. "The biggest bank loan we could get was only $15,000," says Thornton. "And I had to spend $4,000 of that just to secure the place. There was $1,200 for an iron window gate, $400 for an ultrasonic alarm, and the rest went for reinforcing the walls and roof against possible break-in. That's a lot of bread." Before the store was completely secured, Thornton had his first burglary. "It came after an open house," he grimaces. "Along with the other guests, some of my 'brothers' came in, cased the store, then a few nights later cut through the roof and stole two-thirds of my inventory." Because Thornton cannot get insurance, he now sleeps in the back of his store with a sawed-off shotgun, a .38-cal. revolver, and a German shepherd police dog. He calls his place "Dodge City." "You've got a special kind of group ethic working here in the ghetto," explains W. Scott McGilvray III, a young, intense Levi Strauss executive temporarily assigned to Haas' NAB activity. "Regardless of who you are—if you got it, you got it made, and you're ripe to be ripped off [looted]—brother or no brother."

*Fire sale.* Of the dozen minority retail operations which Levi Strauss has helped organize, none were fraught with more problems than the one which fills the company with the greatest satisfaction. That was the transfer to minority ownership of Al's Men's Shop, the Oakland clothing store where Poindexter worked before joining Levi Strauss. After eight months of agonizingly slow negotiations, the deal was finally sealed: four minority employees of the store came up with $6,000, and J. Barth & Co., a San Francisco brokerage and investment house, agreed to provide the equity required to get a $60,000 loan from the "Opportunity through Ownership" consortium. Then less than 30 days before the actual transfer, a fire gutted the store. "After we picked ourselves up" says Poindexter, "we began trying to pick the pieces up. Brother, it was slow."

In the end, the owner agreed to rebuild the store if Levi Strauss would guarantee the lease for five years. To assure continuity, both the original owner and Poindexter also agreed to help manage the store for a year. Then came more trouble. Suppliers who had offered credit for years to the white owner suddenly demanded cash on delivery of the new black owners. "One company we had been dealing with for seven years," says Poindexter, "wouldn't even authorize its salesman to show us their line." The same thing happened with insurance. Two days before the opening, the broker handling the store's coverage notified Poindexter that no company would take the policy. "It's a nice new building and nice new sprinkler system," the broker said. "But it's the same old neighborhood." So Haas picked up the telephone, and "persuaded" an insurer that handles his company to handle the store, as well. "This deal was so full of peaks and valleys," sighs

Poindexter, "we didn't know half the time whether we were up or down." The store finally opened in November of 1969.

As part of its black ownership program, Levi Strauss is also underwriting a minority manufacturer who might eventually supply some of these retailers—and perhaps even compete with Levi Strauss. The company is Ghettos, Inc., a small community organization in Berkeley. Under contract with Levi Strauss, Ghettos produces everything from tote bags and telephone book covers to simple skirts for the Levi's for Gals Div. "At first," says Glasgow, "they wanted to start out big with 50 machine operators and build to 100 in a few weeks. We suggested they start out with two. As it was, they had trouble with just two." They had many other snags, as well—including a phone bill that one month alone ran $322. "The phone was too accessible," Glasgow explains. "Apparently, everybody in the neighborhood was using it." Walter Haas, Jr. has high hopes for the company, however. "They turned their first profit after six months," he says, "and that's certainly encouraging—whatever problems they still have."

## A Frustration With Stereotypes and Attitudes

As a company president who, by long choice, lives on the cutting edge of the social problem, Haas admits that the frustrations are enormous. But they are small compared with the frustrations that he and those around him feel with white businessmen who are not similarly involved. Among the most frustrated and most vocal of his executives is McGilvray—who, in his appearance and zeal, resembles a bearded Bobby Kennedy. "Everywhere you go," McGilvray complains, "you run into the same stereotyped frame of reference. Most whites have never thought of the black man except as a welfare recipient or rock thrower on television. When a black man comes in for a job or a bank loan, they don't know what to do. Hell, we have people literally starving to death. And what do we get? An 'Opportunity through Ownership' consortium with only $2-million to loan—when Bank of America alone has $24-billion in assets. This is a pittance. This is game playing."

In the spring of 1969, McGilvray and Poindexter took their gripes to a New York "Urban Action" conference staged by the American Management Assn. There, they literally broke up the meeting when they stood up and began firing questions at Roger Lewis, chairman and president of General Dynamics Corp. and at that time chairman of the Plans for Progress equal-opportunity program. Would General Dynamics open ghetto-based plants to create jobs? Was General Dynamics ready to help black entrepreneurs? Was the company developing any black suppliers? "Lewis evaded every question," says McGilvray. "He really blew it." Then someone else asked Lewis how many blacks his company had hired. Lewis did not know but said he would stand on his company's record. "At that point," says McGilvray, "this tall, stocky black guy stood up, said he worked for Raytheon, was one of 50,000 employees, and that he was the only black manager. 'So don't tell me you stand on your record,' he told Lewis. Then somebody else rose and suggested that if Lewis did not know how many blacks his company had hired, then he was not qualified to be chairman of Plans for Progress."

*Time for alterations.* The challenge which industry—and the country—faces today is not really social change and pressures, Haas feels. It is the white attitude toward that change and those pressures. And altering these attitudes, Haas says, is where the real challenge lies. "Some of my friends," he notes, "have said they have plenty of job openings for qualified minority people but can't find anyone to fill them. Or they say they've tried hiring some minorities and after a couple of days they didn't show up. These are no longer valid excuses." Haas insists that it is now time "to undertake the expense and training programs necessary to make the unqualified, qualified. People will have to be put into jobs for which they are unprepared. They will have to be taught work habits they have never known. Their associates will have to overlook mistakes and give them far more help than they have ever given a beginner. Business will have to support black businessmen. It will have to encourage black suppliers. This will take patience and time and trouble and money. But unfortunately, there is just no other way."

# 4

# Western Electric Co.

*"We felt we were in a unique position to help"*

OTHO "BUD" McMANUS—26, black, tenth-grade dropout, 15 previous jobs, 20 brushes with the law—sat at a drawing board in the Western Electric Co. plant in Winston-Salem, N.C. It was the spring of 1969, and to hear McManus talk it was also the springtime of what up to then had been a bleak and wintry life. "Look," he told a visitor, "I've had every kind of job that anybody in my neighborhood ever had. Hospital orderly, hotel handyman—you name it. But of all the things I've done, what I'm doing right now is the most important. You know, I never had a real trade before."

McManus was a technical illustrator. Each morning, he settled down at his board and began deftly manipulating a device called a Leroy scriber. With it he produced immaculate, detailed technical instructions for other Western Electric employees. By the summer of 1969, McManus had left Western Electric and moved on to job number 17—but a skilled job that he could probably never have landed without his Western Electric experience. "We hate to lose anyone with promise," says Harold Hill, who had been McManus' supervisor and instructor. "But then again in Bud's case, you get a feeling of satisfaction in that you helped push back his horizons a little and that you opened up some job options and opportunities that he might not otherwise have had."

*Varied approach.*   As the manufacturing and supply arm of the Bell system and the recipient of one of two 1969 *Business Week* citizenship awards for "human resources," Western Electric has been pushing back minority horizons all over the country. "With facilities in 30 states and a purchasing function that deals with 47,000 suppliers in 50 states," says William G. Chaffee, vice president, "we felt we were in a unique position to help." The company has pioneered new approaches in hiring and training the disadvantaged. It is moving into education. It is developing black suppliers. It is helping other small minority businessmen get started. It is also providing leadership for community-wide efforts.

Along the way, Western Electric has run into a pack of problems, and is a long way from solving some of them. But the company is pressing ahead and—unlike many of its colleagues in industry—no longer regards the American buying public as a fairytale cow that is fed in heaven and milked on earth. This particular cow, as Western Electric learned first-hand at some of its inner-city locations, is quite capable of kicking over the lantern and setting the whole barn on fire. For that reason, the company has made social involvement part of its day-to-day business, and lives by a sort of Gresham's Law governing all social improvement efforts—that is, that soft promises only drive out hard performance. Western Electric stresses performance over promises, and has bucked the word all the way down its executive line.

## A Picture of Social Injustices

Winston-Salem is one example where the word stuck. A part of the scenic Piedmont Crescent, Winston-Salem is a small (pop.: 142,000), quiet picturesque city with rolling hills and historic restorations that make it a vacationer's delight. Wake Forest University makes its home there, as do many nationally-known tobacco, textile, and furniture firms. But in the summer of 1967, the city received a far different picture of itself. In a report prepared for the mayor by a task force working under Western Electric's Kenneth A. Johnson, manager of industrial and labor relations, the city was put on notice that it faced "immediate, mid-range, and long-range problems in remedying the consequences of old social injustices and in upgrading our labor potential for the competitive future." There was hope, however. "These problems are manageable and can be solved," the report indicated. "Our community possesses the agencies, the men, and the money, as well as the brains, enlightened self-interest, and sense of community responsibility necessary to achieve success."

*Prescription for change.* Johnson's report made several recommendations. Among them was one proposing a new office in City Hall—special assistant to the mayor on manpower problems. The first man to hold the job was John Dawson, Western Electric's manager of community relations. "When we started work," says Dawson, "we found that the local agencies designed to attack these problems were uncoordinated, and that their efforts overlapped and often duplicated each other. They were hardly making a dent." Dawson became a liaison man among the agencies and, in turn, between the agencies and industry—the man who could open doors, cut through red tape, make decisions, and tie the loose ends of public and private social efforts into a reasonably neat bow.

Another task force recommendation that was adopted called for an industry job-training program. For one typical class, Western Electric contributed the materials, two instructors, and the services of two other employees who designed the curriculum. With evident satisfaction, Dawson recalls how the plan, which was to cost the government only $400 per trainee, "captured the attention of Dept. of Labor officials. They were accustomed to training costs of $2,500 to $3,000 per trainee."

A third proposal by Johnson's task force also caught on—an idea for a "Concentrated Employment Program," which was to become the manpower arm of the city's anti-poverty agency. Today, CEP offers the disadvantaged one-stop service in counseling, medical and legal aid, day care, training, and job placement. "Beyond putting people to work and helping them cope with some of their problems," says James Bond, CEP's acting head and deputy director of the local anti-poverty agency, "we're in the much more basic business of taking people who are dependent on society and making them contributors to that society. This means changing attitudes, outlook, and fundamental human relationships, and I think we are succeeding at that."

*Up from complacency.* Western Electric's Johnson, who became president of the city's anti-poverty agency, feels his own relationships and perspectives have changed almost as much. "Eight or ten years ago," he says, "I was pretty complacent—aloof—about these things. I was like a lot of people—guilty of oversimplifying the problems." But when he joined in the city-wide job drive, "I began to get excited about actually doing something." Adds Western Electric's Dawson: "As company employment manager, I used to insist on a high school diploma as a minimum qualification. Now I've learned that a diploma is utterly irrelevant for some jobs."

## *"Career Fair," Coaching, and the ABC'S*

In Kansas City, local Western Electric executives took on some of the same problems and went through the same change in outlook. "We in industry," says one, "have had our heads in the sand too long." At its Kansas City (Mo.) Works, Western Electric is recruiting and training more than 60 disadvantaged workers, and for the last two summers has hired 20 underprivileged high school youngsters as temporary help. In addition, Floyd Lubert, local personnel manager, went on loan to the Kansas City branch of the National Alliance of Businessmen and served full-time in 1968, as job procurement manager. Three other Western Electric employees came over with him, rotating as his assistant. At the same time, Western Electric's James Hosford, then works manager in Kansas City, headed up the local Urban Coalition.

As part of a community drive, Hosford, Lubert, and other Western Electric executives worked with the Urban League and Chamber of Commerce to organize a "Career Fair" for the disadvantaged. Its aim: to keep younger students from dropping out of school and to help graduating seniors and any unemployed or underemployed parents land a job. "Response was greater than expected," says fair co-chairman Fred Fuller, an operating supervisor with Western Electric. Some 8,000 ninth-graders from 23 Kansas City area schools attended two daytime sessions, and another 5,000 high school seniors and parents showed up for night sessions.

One ninth-grader was so enthusiastic about the daytime phase that he returned that evening with his underemployed father in tow. Other students were more mistrustful. "Nobody believed there would be any jobs," one girl said. "We decided they'd probably just tear up our applications." Explained a local teacher: "They've heard so many promises, only to have nothing happen. Now when they see you coming, they have a deaf ear."

The only way to change such an attitude, says Lubert, is for business to deliver the goods. "If we don't," he warns, "there's no hope. We have to prove to the Negro community and to everyone else that we're sincere. Any delay will only reinforce years of mistrust."

*Safety valve.* To help keep ghetto youngsters off the streets, Lubert also spearheaded the formation of the Inner City Coaches Council, a group of 16 volunteer coaches and 16 assistants who work out with disadvantaged youngsters at local schools. With his industry and government contacts, Lubert arranged for the Council to hire a full-time paid secretary, aided in setting up federal funding, and even came up with desks, typewriters, filing cabinets, and other supplies.

During one recent summer evening at the city's Central and Southeast High Schools, hundreds of young men splashed in the school swimming pools and scrambled around the basketball courts. "Our objective here," Central's basketball coach James Wilkinson said, "is to keep these boys busy at night, to make the competition good enough so that when they leave here they're tired. Tired kids go home. They don't go looking for trouble . . ." Out on the court, several boys started roughing it up. So Wilkinson went bounding across the floor. "Some of the boys you just watched," he said later outside the gym, "were in deep trouble when we had five people killed in the 1967 riot. Several of the kids were involved in fires and looting. Just the other night I asked one young boy what he'd be doing if he weren't here with us, and he said he'd be out on the street stealing. Things like that make me feel we're accomplishing what we set out to do in this program." As the gym lights flickered off that evening at 9:30, the boys trooped out into the humid night air—laughing, joking, and suitably exhausted.

By that time of night, most of Western Electric's 20 student summer workers were also ready for bed—considering their 5 a.m. rising time. "Although most of them have never worked before, they are doing very well," Theodore Merrell, assistant manager in charge of the program, said. "We try to leave them alone and it works because as a group these kids are very sharp, and used to taking care of themselves." Their transportation is one example. "We've contracted with a school bus company," Merrell explained, "to pick them up at three locations each morning and take them back at night. Each student pays $1.35 a day out of what he earns. We could pay it, but this way each of them gets an added sense of responsibility."

*Breaking down defenses.* In Los Angeles, the Western Electric Service Center organized a similar bus system for its disadvantaged trainees—and threw in one added bonus. Because the workers were high school dropouts, the company provided some basic schooling, along with its vocational training. In a program initiated in March of 1968 and coordinated with the Youth Training and Employment Project, eight trainees were taught math and English by YTEP's Gladstone Fairweather. "I would push and laugh, push and laugh," Fairweather says, explaining his efforts at building rapport. "Sometimes I was hard on them. Once they wouldn't speak to me for two days."

Part of their education included an "industrial orientation" to shape attitudes, work habits, behavior, dress, and relations with co-workers. During one phase, the counselor acted as interviewer, a trainee played the role of job applicant, and the rest of the group evaluated the trainee's performance. Their comments were pointed:

> "Don't look away so much. Look the man in the eye."
> "Talk more clearly."

After a while, the trainees were fielding questions with finesse:

> "What would you do if you couldn't get along with your supervisor?"
> "Talk over the problem with him. I wouldn't get hostile."

"What if he won't talk about it?"

"I'd go to a higher authority."

The trainees were eased into their new jobs like it was a piping hot bath. They began by watching other employees. Then for two hours they started working on the training line—but without the conveyor running. Then they finally went to work. Early counseling sessions showed that some of the men remained painfully unsure of their surroundings. "At first," says Al Nichols, a YTEP counselor, "they just stared and wouldn't speak. The second day I discussed the situation with them, and they admitted they were being too defensive. After that, they began to adjust." By the fourth week of the five-week training period, their production and quality were up to that of experienced employees.

## Flagship Effort in Newark

The same week that Western Electric launched its Los Angeles program, the company began another job-training experiment in Newark—one that went on to become a sort of flagship effort within the company and one of industry's biggest single programs of its kind. This was the opening of a satellite or "vestibule" plant on the edge of Newark's riot-scarred Central Ward. "We realized," says James J. Doherty, Newark-based manufacturing vice president for cable and wire products, "that we had all the components of the national urban problem right here in our midst. There was a startling increase in the black and Spanish-American population. There was also an equal increase in tax burden caused by the retreat of tax-paying businesses to the suburbs and by an ever-expanding number of disadvantaged people on welfare. Unemployment, crime, and communicable disease rates were among the highest in the nation." From the company's experience in other plants, "we already knew that these individuals could be trained to do the job. Their problem was getting in the door."

*Ahead of target.* Western Electric's decision to open the door was part of a one-year Bell system commitment to provide 550 jobs for the disadvantaged—primarily Negro and Puerto Rican residents of New Jersey's inner cities. Western Electric set a goal of 250 jobs for Newark-area residents who could not meet regular entry requirements—for instance, a high school diploma, good health, absence of a criminal record. Today, the "Newark Shops," as they are called, operate out of a converted automobile showroom, and offer training in everything from cable forming and key-punch operation to telephone installation and repair. By mid-November of 1969, the company had considered 597 applicants and hired 440. Of those hired, 99 were still in training, 171 had graduated to "mainstream" or regular jobs with Western Electric, and the rest—roughly 40% of the original hirees—had either dropped out or been dismissed. "This puts us ahead of our earlier projections," says Doherty. "We figured if we achieved a 50% flow-through, we could count the program a success."

Chronic absenteeism and lateness remain the biggest problems—and the most common reasons for dismissal. "Teaching job skills is only 25% of the job," Doherty feels. Teaching the "industrial discipline"—regular and punctual attendance—is "75% of it." Absenteeism, however, is not always a matter of goofing off. "On a rainy day," says section supervisor Donald Williams, "I can always expect poor attendance. You'd be surprised how many of these people don't have umbrellas or raincoats." Doherty tells the story of the Spanish-American trainee who was constantly late for work. "We looked into the problem," he recalls, "and discovered that these Spanish-American families are very closely knit—something I didn't know before. And because this particular employee was the only family member with a car, he was always chauffeuring his brothers, sisters, aunts, uncles, and everybody else. It just never dawned on him or them that he was sacrificing $2.30 an hour. So now, they take cabs and he comes to work." Another supervisor solved a punctuality problem by simply buying the trainee an alarm clock.

*Beyond the mainstream.*   After punctuality, the next worst problem is lack of education—which, in turn, often leads to employee frustration. The company recently tested some of its employees at the Newark Shops and found that 61% scored below the national norms for the eighth grade. "We know," Doherty says, "that the expectations of these employees go beyond 'graduation' to a mainstream job. But how can they progress without more basic education?" The company offers tuition refunds for those with a high school diploma, and another program leads to a high school equivalency certificate. The problem, Doherty says, is that "We don't yet have a program for those not ready for high school equivalency study. But in looking at the broad problem, the question is how far should we, as a company, try to go?" One mainstream department chief feels this issue of advancement is "the real question." Disadvantaged trainees who graduate to mainstream jobs, he says, "can do a lot to help themselves. It will be up to them."

## An Incentive For Success

Typical of those minority employees who have helped themselves and have made it at Western Electric is Charles E. Jones. A management-level instructor in Western Electric's Corporate Education Center in Princeton, N.J., Jones is the first Negro graduate of the company's Lehigh University masters degree program, a fully accredited course open to company engineers who show "outstanding" ability.

*Reinforced frustration.*   Jones came up the hard way—from Huntsville, Ala., where his mother was a domestic and his father died when he was four. "There were the poor people," he says with a wry grin, "and then there were the people the poor considered poor. That was my situation." If you wanted a job, he recalls, "you just went somewhere and hung around. You pitched in with the work and sooner or later they'd start paying you." Jones sent himself through grade school working at a mattress factory, where he had just "pitched in." Later, he worked summers chopping and picking cotton. "There's nothing like cotton," he says, "to make you want an education."

And there was nothing like "the system" to frustrate that education. "At least five times a day," he recalls, "you had to acknowledge the system—when you used the men's room, when you wanted a drink, when you went to a restaurant. It was almost like a religion, continually reinforced." Jones recalls a professor at predominantly Negro Alabama A&M telling him that he might get a job when he graduated and—if he were lucky—he might even earn almost as much as a white university graduate. "I felt sick," he says. "The man who was telling me this had a Ph.D. It's one thing to be a second class citizen but to see a man with a Ph.D. accept the fact that he is—that is something." Jones later went on to Michigan State University, studied electrical engineering, and began participating in the civil rights movement. After joining Western Electric in 1963, he continued his ghetto activities in Chicago and now in Trenton, where he makes his home. Today, he works with a Trenton community group that is rehabilitating drug addicts. "I used to be naive enough to believe in the ultimate good," he says. "When the nation really knew what the situation was, the people would make it go away. This is a romantic notion. We cannot love our problems away."

*Multiple formula.* Jones feels part of the answer is the varied approach which Western Electric takes in its minority hiring. "There is no one single formula that will be all things to all people in all cities," he stresses. "So we must try a lot of things and experiment with a lot of approaches." Western Electric has certainly done that. Besides those efforts described in Winston-Salem, Kansas City, Los Angeles, and Newark, Western Electric also:

- Provides part-time employment and on-the-job training for Arlington, Va. high school juniors and seniors.
- Expanded its in-plant high school program to six locations, enabling dropouts to pick up a diploma.
- Offers special on-the-job training and remedial education at its Buffalo plant.
- Conducts an eight-week evening course in data processing for underprivileged high school students in Denver.
- Provides after-hours volunteer tutors for an inner-city elementary school in Aurora, Ill.
- Supplies professional guidance and counseling for disadvantaged Newark high school sophomores and juniors who want to go into engineering.
- Created Volunteers in Action, a sort of private Peace Corps in which Western Electric and other Bell system employees in New York City, Winston-Salem, and Newark tutor or guide the underprivileged in education, employment training, counseling, and personal motivation.
- Set up a satellite plant, patterned on the Newark Shops, in Baltimore, where the company is geared to train 40 to 50 disadvantaged workers (*v.* 120 in Newark).
- Organized a welding instruction program, a cooperative effort of Western Electric's Omaha Works, Northwestern Bell Telephone Co., and the Omaha Opportunities Industrialization Center.
- Participates in an industry metal-working training program, focusing on the Greater Newark area and combining three weeks of basic education (math, communications arts, attitudinal training) with six weeks of instruction in machine shop skills.
- Cooperates with the Urban League in Arizona, New York, Utah, and Oregon, and helps minority groups improve their em-

ployability by developing basic clerical skills and employment techniques.

■ Set up a special program in Atlanta, Nashville, and Miami, training the disadvantaged as beginning installers.

*Ultimate proof.* Beyond jobs, Western Electric also recognizes a need for more help to the small black businessman. "In the end," says Western Electric's Jones, "the example of the successful black businessman may be the best incentive for the Negro youngster. This gives him a reason for staying in school, setting some goals, and trying to work toward them. It provides proof that the black man can make it."

After the Detroit riots in 1967, Western Electric mounted a major effort to help develop black entrepreneurs. As a starter, the company signed the first of $60,000 worth of contracts with Watts Mfg. Co., a black-managed subsidiary of Aerojet-General Corp. Since then, Western Electric has lined up more than 70 other minority suppliers in a dozen cities, often providing management assistance, training, and sometimes start-up capital. To help such suppliers broaden their base, the company also sponsored—along with several local groups—three suppliers' fairs just for black businessmen. Two were staged in Chicago, one in New York. The latest, held in Chicago's International Amphitheatre in September of 1969, drew 510 black suppliers and purchasing agents from 148 companies representing more than $100-million worth of annual purchasing power in the Chicago area. Among the buyers: General Motors Corp., Ford Motor Co., Montgomery Ward & Co., Sears, Roebuck Co., Admiral Corp., and, of course, Western Electric. The total sales run up by the three fairs: more than $1-million.

At the first Chicago fair, Cecil Carmickle, who operates a building and remodelling company, voiced the frustrations that many small Negro suppliers feel today. "There is a lot of small contracting work to be done," he noted. The problem is making that first, big contact. "If you don't know anyone," he asked, "how do you get in?" Entrepreneur James Watts, who heads up Chicago's Impac Chemical Products Co., said he made contacts at the fair that would normally take "three to four years." There is the added value, another small supplier said, "that black businessmen can deal directly with white businessmen. There is no government agency or program."

Buyers were just as enthusiastic. "We met more minority businessmen today than we have in several years," one purchasing agent marvelled. "They should be encouraged to call on the larger firms more often."

## Developing Communication on Both Sides

A lot of other things should be encouraged, as well. And a lot more things should be done. "We had hoped," says one Western Electric executive, "that what we are doing—both in hardcore hiring and in promoting black entrepreneurship—would stimulate other companies to do as much or more. This is not always happening, and it concerns us."

Speaking for Western Electric and the rest of the Bell system, H. I. Romnes, board chairman of American Telephone & Telegraph Co., suggests that some companies—even those deeply involved in social good works—are suffering from a lack of vision. Attacking ghetto problems themselves, he feels, is only half the solution. The other half is developing a full comprehension on the part of whites of just what those problems are, why they are important, and why the business community—both management and employees, as well—should be doing more. "Employees must know what the ills of the core city portend," says Romnes. "They must know the acuteness of the problems of the poor. They must sense the dangers that neglect will aggravate. They must increase their understanding of the Negro—his history, his environment, his attitudes, his potential. In short, we must communicate, learn, and understand among ourselves if we are to communicate with the community through significant, creative social action."

For a company whose business is communication, Western Electric is well on its way.

# 5

# American Metal Climax, Inc.

*"Keeping the land unspoiled"*

THERE COMES A TIME when every red-blooded American male is tempted, in H. L. Mencken's words, "to spit on his hands, hoist the black flag, and begin slitting throats." Many conservationists feel that way today. "In years past when we had a problem with industry," says Roger Hansen, executive director of the Colorado Open Space Foundation, "we tried to settle it over a conference table. Then if that failed we brought pressure and if that failed we went to court. Now many groups start out assuming that business won't cooperate, and they are increasingly going straight to court."

One company that is cooperating—and to an almost unrivaled degree—is American Metal Climax, Inc., a $600-million natural resources developer and the recipient of one of two 1969 *Business Week* citizenship awards for contributions to the "physical environment." In the heart of the Colorado Rockies 50 miles west of Denver, the Climax Molybdenum Co., a division of AMAX, is developing two new molybdenum mines and along the way is proving that conservationists and industry—if not always agreeing—can at least sit down together, reason through their differences, and develop a constructive dialogue. Ian MacGregor, board chairman and chief executive officer of AMAX, insists that "the goals of conservation are compatible with full utilization of our mineral resources." He has also said: "We must learn to make multiple use of the land—mining and processing nature's riches in order to maintain our high standard of living, while keeping the land and our environment unspoiled for the enjoyment of the citizens of today and the generations of tomorrow." What MacGregor has not said—but what is implicit in everything that AMAX is doing—is that snowballing public pressures make any other position tenuous at best and economically suicidal at worst.

*New problems and approaches.* Environmental control is nothing new for AMAX. In the past, the company has been widely recognized for its anti-pollution efforts at a copper smelter and refinery in New Jersey, an aluminum reduction plant in the State of Washington, and a lead mine, mill, and smelter in Southeast Missouri. But in Colorado, AMAX ran into special problems—and special pressures—that required a fresh approach. The two new Colorado facilities, the $30-million Urad mine and the far larger $200-million Henderson mine, have total estimated ore reserves of 315-million tons. Collectively, that puts them second only to the division's huge mine at Climax, Colo., which now turns out 50% of the free world's total molybdenum supply and has remaining ore reserves estimated at more than 400-million tons. The trouble with the two new mines was that they had unusual problems of topography and both are located in Red Mountain, where they straddle National Forest land in a prime recreation area.

"With a situation like that," says James Gilliland, director of environmental control for Climax Molybdenum, "no conservationist was about to sit idly by. So we decided to go out, meet them halfway, and try to anticipate their demands."

## Subterranean Plumbing for Two Creeks

To understand the environmental problems that Climax Molybdenum ran into, you have to understand the mechanics of molybdenum mining and processing. Once the ore is dug out of the mine, it goes through several crushing and pulverizing steps that grind it down to the consistency of sand. Then the molybdenum is separated out by water flotation, and the waste—finely ground rock which leaves the mill as a muddy slime—is piped into "tailing ponds" adjacent to the mill. There, the "tailing" or solid waste settles to the bottom, and the water re-circulates back to the mill for re-use. What sets the conservationists off is not only the fact of the mine and mill as interlopers into nature areas. Conservationists also fret over the enormous amount of waste generated in molybdenum mining. For every 2,000 lb. of ore dug out of Red Mountain, there will be 1,992 lb. of waste once the ore is processed. Before the Urad and Henderson properties are exhausted, in other words, more than 310-million tons of waste will have to be disposed of.

At the Urad mine, which went into production in 1967, there was the added problem that the ore body lay about 1,100 ft. above the floor of a narrow valley. That meant that the valley floor would have to be filled and raised in order to make room for the mine's surface facilities. "And that, in turn, meant that unless we took special control measures," says Edwin Eisenach, Climax Molybdenum's vice president of Western operations, "two streams that ran through the valley would be seriously polluted by the tailing ponds and our other mine operations." Before filling in the valley, therefore, company engineers installed 2 mi. of reinforced, 6-ft. dia. concrete pipe on the valley floor. Then on top of this went 300,000 yards of earth fill. Today, Urad's special plumbing carries the two creeks under the work site and deposits them in their normal stream beds below the mine area.

*Multi-purpose reservoir.*   As part of its water-pollution control, Climax Molybdenum also designed a series of four dams— two just below the mine and mill site to create tailing ponds for waste, another downstream to catch and store the water that seeps out of the two tailing ponds, and a fourth double-purpose dam up above the mine and mill. This fourth dam acts as a reservoir both to catch and hold the mine's fresh water supply, and also provide a special recreation area for outdoors-loving residents. In preparing the reservoir site, the company stripped away all debris and tree snags, had the Colorado Game, Fish, and Parks Dept. stock the water with trout, built a road for quick, easy access, and invited the public in to camp and fish. For winter sportsmen who want to brave the area's bone-chilling temperatures and try out their snow shoes and snowmobiles, the company added a special parking lot just below the mining area.

In the crisp, thin air of the Rockies, Robert Kendrick, mine "super" at Urad, recently leaned against his durable, four-wheel drive pickup and waved an arm at the rolling mountainscape before him. "You can't work properties like this," he said, "and not want to continue, somehow, sharing them with the public. We get maybe 2,000 or 3,000 people up here every year. In a way, we've even made the area more accessible, and with our upstream reservoir, perhaps even more recreational."

## An "Experiment in Ecology"

At Urad, all development work and future plans are continually studied by an eagle-eyed battery of state and federal officials, including the Bureau of Land Management, U. S. Fish and Wildlife Service, Colorado Game, Fish, and Parks Dept., U. S. Forest Service, and State Bureau of Mines. At the company's nearby Henderson mine—scheduled for production in the mid-1970s— Climax Molybdenum went one important step further: it established a formal working relationship with the Colorado Open Space Foundation, a large private conservation group.

*Attempt at short-circuiting.* The joint Climax Molybdenum-COSF undertaking, dubbed "Experiment in Ecology," traces its roots back to 1965. In that year, the "action" arm of COSF, the Colorado Open Space Council, hooked up with the Colorado Assn. of Commerce and Industry and organized a joint committee of businessmen and conservationists. "This was an attempt," says COSF's Roger Hansen, a co-chairman of the committee, "to understand each other's position and philosophy and see if we could establish some kind of meeting ground between the citizen conservation movement and industry."

Among the other committee members was Stanley Dempsey, division attorney for Climax Molybdenum and a hardy outdoorsman and longtime mountaineer. "At the time I joined the committee," says Dempsey, "neither I nor most other people at the company knew we were about to develop the Henderson reserves. I joined the committee mostly out of my own personal interest in conservation." Then when Dempsey got wind of the company's plans for Henderson, he met with Hansen one evening in a Denver cocktail lounge and casually sounded him out on an idea. Would COSF, he asked, be willing to participate in the planning and development of a mining property? Hansen agreed to think about it. Working with Robert Venuti—assistant director of operations for the Denver Research Institute and, at that time, president of COSF—Hansen drafted a long proposal and submitted it to Climax Molybdenum.

At that point—before anyone was committed—both sides did some deep soul-searching. "There's nothing more dangerous for a conservationist," notes Hansen, "than to appear to be crawling into bed with industry." Echoes William Distler, project manager at Henderson: "We were in the same ticklish spot. Within our industry, other companies look at you and say, 'Ah hah, you're giving in. Now you're going to do everything they want,' " Such a project would also mean making COSF privy to confidential information on mining costs and operations. "And at that particular time," Distler notes, "we weren't even sure we wanted to disclose that we planned to develop Henderson—let alone throw the property open to a bunch of conservationists." On Climax Molybdenum's part, the final decision went all the way up to MacGregor.

*A gingerly grip.*   Once both sides decided to go ahead, a joint committee was formed. On the conservationists' side, there were Hansen, Venuti, Dr. E. Robert Weiner, associate professor of chemistry at the University of Denver and now president of COSF, and Dr. Beatrice Willard, an ecologist and vice president of Boulder's respected Thorne Ecological Foundation. From Climax Molybdenum, there were Dempsey, Distler, Eisenach, and Donald Stephens, Eisenach's assistant. "All of us," Venuti recalls, "had strong doubts at first." Adds Dr. Willard: "We didn't know what was going to happen. Everyone was holding on gingerly, willing to let go whenever things got too hot."

The first few meetings, however, went smoothly. The conservationists accepted the idea that there was going to be a mine, and that their wisest course of action was to try to talk Climax Molybdenum into taking steps to protect the environment. Climax Molybdenum, in turn, recognized that it was better to have the conservationists with them rather than against them. A few weeks after the committee came into being, Climax Molybdenum organized the first joint field trip to the Henderson site. "Of course," Dempsey recalls, "the company wanted to put everything in the best possible light. So we shepherded our visitors to this beautiful valley, delivered this long spiel about how it would have been cheaper to put our facilities there rather than somewhere else, but that we decided to preserve this lovely area. Bob Weiner just looked at me and said: 'Fine. Now that we have seen the area you have miraculously saved, let's go see the area you're going to screw up.' " In those early stages, Weiner says with a grin, he felt the conservationists should be "skeptical in a constructive way."

*Color-coordinating.* By whatever name, the cooperative effort is working. To heal over some of the land scars that its operations will create, Climax Molybdenum is experimenting with a kind of instant grass-maker—a mulching machine that spews fertilizer and seed against a cut embankment or tailing area and makes it sprout, if not exactly bloom. In the design of its buildings, the company is using colored siding rather than the usual, drab galvanized steel. This way, the buildings can be color-coordinated with their surroundings. Some 6,000 acres of woodland have been thrown open for hunting, hiking, and camping. And wherever possible, of course, engineers are trying to preserve the natural environment. Max Gelwix, chief engineer for Climax Molybdenum's Western Operations, admits that he would have planned the whole project differently 10 or 20 years ago. "But an engineer has to recognize the needs of the country and the temperament of the times," he says. "And there's been a tremendous change in temperament in the last 10 years." Even his construction workers are entering into the spirit of the project. Dr. Willard recalls some of the workers going to the chief engineer one day and telling him they were going to re-route the road slightly to save six trees. "It's not a big thing," she says. "But when you consider what they usually do, it was quite something." Weiner recalls workers clearing land for the processing plant. "On their own," he says, "they brought trees out by horse so they wouldn't even have to build a road."

Climax Molybdenum's biggest concession to the environment, however, came in its method for handling tailing. For the sake of convenience, tailing is normally stored near the mine. At Henderson, that would have put it within a short eagle's glide of a major highway. Therefore, company engineers are tunnelling 9.3 mi. through Red Mountain, building a 13-mi. railroad at a cost of $25-million, and placing their mill and tailing pond far from the public's—and conservationists'—view. In designing the railroad, engineers took extra pains to avoid fencing off deer and elk migration trails, leading down to the lowlands. "Above the pond," adds Distler, "we are also planning a series of flood control canals to guarantee that run-off water from the mountains doesn't sweep down through the pond and pollute the area and its natural streams."

To keep winter snow build-ups from doing the same thing—and wiping out huge stands of forests, as well as any buildings in their path—Climax Molybdenum maintains an "avalanche control engineer" named Den Davidson. Davidson and his assistant spend most of the winter traveling around the mining areas, "shooting" avalanches with a converted baseball-pitching machine. Davidson's machine lobs a blasting agent into dangerous-looking snow build-ups. This diverts and neutralizes them by controlling the direction they come skidding down the mountain. Avalanche forecasting is still more art than science," Davidson admits. "We can predict avalanche probability through measurements of snow density and shear strength. Unfortunately, we can't crystal-ball precisely where or when a slide will run." As an equally unfortunate result, Davidson has been buried four times—but always returns to shoot again.

## A Profounder Understanding—on Both Sides

Just as important as the environmental control measures that have come out of "Experiment in Ecology" is the rare communication and depth of understanding that has developed between Climax Molybdenum and the conservationists. After working closely together, both sides have acquired perspective and a keen appreciation—though not always sympathy—for the position of the other side.

As part of their mutual education the conservationists traveled with their AMAX counterparts to Arizona and spent three days visiting mines and studying reclamation projects. Then in both 1967 and 1968, Dempsey and several other Climax Molybdenum executives joined the conservationists and attended the annual "Seminar on Environmental Arts and Sciences," sponsored in Aspen by the Thorne Ecological Foundation. There, the Climax Molybdenum executives acquired a real, if somewhat rarified, taste of what conservation and ecology are all about—from the conservationists' viewpoint.

*Search for answers.* Hansen recalls the excitement of a typical seminar field trip. "Look at the landscape," he thrills. "What is a landscape? What is in the landscape? Cast out the prejudices, the preconceptions. Observe. Think. Tune your senses to a higher frequency. Look at the scrub oak on the slopes above a steep, winding dirt road. The leaves are dead. Why? Are dandelions better than roses? There is a 'gopher garden.' Does the gopher serve any 'useful function?' What does the gopher give? What does he take away? Is there a 'good' or a 'bad' in nature? High above us, new ski trails slither down the mountainside. Freshly-cut brush is burning—gray smoke on blue sky. How will these trails change the landscape in future years? What about moisture patterns, the effect of high winds on exposed aspen, possible increases in solar radiation? We walk through the woods and come to the pond. How did the pond get here? Did you ever see so many frogs? If big frogs eat little frogs, what do little frogs eat? Is that small flowering plant 'scum' or duckweed? How long will the aspen remain? What will the pond look like in another 200 years? What might man do to the pond? Drain it? Enlarge it? Fill it with water skiers and motorboats? Is 'disturbance' always a negative term or is only man-made disturbance negative?"

To some of the Climax Molybdenum visitors, it was all quite an education. "This was the wildest bunch of people I've ever seen," recalls one company executive. "I thought I'd seen everything until this one fellow in our group got down on his hands and knees and began examining the underside of a daisy."

## The Limits of the Law

Such give-and-take, however, goes a long way. By fostering a greater understanding on both sides, it helps minimize the need for stiffer environmental laws that might accomplish absolutely nothing. "When there is a law hanging over you," says Venuti, "there is a natural tendency just to go so far—to meet the minimum requirement. But when you have both sides talking and working together, you are often prepared to go further, if only because you have some say and flexibility." Venuti cites the case of a junk dealer on Highway 85 north of Denver. "His junkyard was a real eyesore," Venuti notes. "But rather than go to the guy and try to reason with him, everybody got together and passed this law that he had to put a fence up. Well, he did. But because of the nature of the terrain, the fence really didn't screen off the mess that much. The result is that the dealer has complied with the law, laid out $7,000 or $8,000, and is burned up as hell— where maybe some of us could have gone in there and gotten him to do more on his own hook. Now, he won't talk with anyone."

Venuti feels the pressures that conservationists can generate are much more potent that any regulations could ever be. In the case of Climax Molybdenum's Henderson mine, Venuti claims the company would have faced a bruising battle if there had been no meeting of the minds with conservationists. "We as conservationists don't have all that much financial capability," he admits, "and we may not have won in the first two or three years. But we would have lined up citizen support, and 10 or 15 years from now we might have been able to shut down that mine. And Climax Molybdenum knew that."

*Re-examining an ethic.* Where industry refuses to cooperate, of course, there is no choice but tougher regulation. And that could well be on the way, according to Hansen. "Our whole social ethic," he stresses, "is based on the fact that what improves the business climate improves the quality of American life. Therefore, our society tries to produce more and more things, and make them bigger and bigger, and what we don't want, we simply throw away." But now, says Hansen, we are coming to the point where there are fewer and fewer places to throw things away. "That means we must begin altering our social ethic," he feels. "And if industry does not decide to cooperate, then the government will have to decide for it, because we conservationists are going to pressure government the same way we are pressuring business."

Up to now, Hansen claims that conservationists have been far too conservative. "A Los Angeles business executive recently said to me: 'You conservationists are the wave of the future. You are going to win. I don't see how anybody can avoid getting on your bandwagon.' But there is a problem. We don't take advantage of all the favorable conservation climate in America." One reason, he notes, is that conservation organizations are "woefully underfinanced. An annual budget of over $200 is somehow considered immoral. The same individual who gives $100 to his chamber of commerce, $200 to his club, and $300 to his charity calls himself a conservationist—and gives $10 a year to the Sierra Club. In a world of real professionals, we pride ourselves on our amateurism." But now, Hansen feels, there are encouraging signs that the movement is starting to consolidate and think big. As evidence, he points to the success and growth of the Colorado Open Space Council, the four-year-old "action" arm of COSF. COSC brings together in one organization 26 recreational conservation groups representing 30,000 Colorado and Rocky Mountain area residents and nearly every conservation cause from highway beautification and air and water quality to—improbable as it may sound—birth control. As conservationists continue to pick up internal momentum, Hansen warns, industry had better watch out.

*Drawing the line.* On its side, Climax Molybdenum is determined to cooperate as much as possible. "The dividends are too numerous to pass up," says Eisenach. "Whatever you spend, you get it back in improved community relations, in pride of workers on the job, and in the personal satisfaction of having done some small thing to help improve the physical environment." But Climax Molybdenum has drawn the line. "This is, as the name suggests, only an experiment," Eisenach stresses. "Neither we nor COSF are locked into any rigid positions. For obvious reasons, neither of us could afford to be."

In some instances, COSF requested design changes at Henderson that would have involved faulty engineering. The foundation also pushed unsuccessfully for a national institute of industrial ecology, to be located on the Henderson property. "Such an institute," as Hansen describes it, "could provide expert advice to industry on how to avoid stream, air, or general landscape pollution. If a mining company had a reclamation problem, for instance, it could come to the institute, learn what kind of grass to use, and how to plant, water, and fertilize it. Or if it had some design problem, the institute could supply architectural help and assist on colors." Eisenach agrees that such an effort might be worthwhile—but not on the Henderson property, or necessarily at the company's expense. "This is out of the question," he feels. "Because of safety reasons alone, we couldn't assume liability for such a facility."

There are also other matters to be ironed out. COSF's Dr. Willard, for example, wants to do considerably more research on wind patterns around the tailing pond. "If wind lifts the tailing into the air and drops it on plants," she says, "we can have all kinds of problems." Some day, she hopes, conservationists will be able to turn to a handy book of tables and find out that March winds around Henderson average 20 or 30 mph from the Southwest. "Then," she notes, "we could combine that with the specific gravity of molybdenum tailing and see if there is going to be any danger of the tailing polluting the air." Whatever her research shows, there is already one certainty that has come out of "Experiment in Ecology" and the company's other environmental control activities—Climax Molybdenum and AMAX already know which way the wind is blowing.

# 6

## Rouse Co.

*"An environment that serves, rather than dictates".*

"THE PROBLEM OF THE CITY," says James Rouse, his eyes twinkling with excitement, "is not just congestion, pollution, deterioration—nor crime, disease, and rats; nor housing, nor unemployment. It is all of these, of course, but underlying all these conditions are the questions: How did it happen? How did the city get this way? What causes our cities to rot away physically and socially?"

As president of Rouse Co. and a highly successful mortgage banker and master builder, Rouse is now trying to answer his own questions. On 14,000 gently rolling acres in the Maryland countryside, Rouse Co.—recipient of one of two 1969 *Business Week* citizenship awards for contributions to the "physical environment"—is building a self-contained model city on the thesis that the problems of today's city are not so much social or economic, as environmental. When completed in 1980, Columbia, Md.—located midway between Baltimore and Washington—will provide housing for 110,000 people, employment for 30,000, and include 70 schools, 50 churches, a full range of cultural and recreational activities, handy suburban and downtown shopping, and such unusual urban amenities as three scenic stream valleys, 3,000 acres of forests, five lakes, and 26 miles of riding trails.

Above all, says Rouse Vice President William Finley, Columbia will provide maximum convenience and an environment that "serves, rather than dictates." School sites, for instance, have been laid out on the sunniest slopes, since the snow melts soonest there. To help beat that old wifely syndrome known as "suburban blues"—the sense of isolation caused when hubby takes the family's only car to work—40% of the homes are within a two-minute walk of a bus-stop, and buses run every five minutes. To safeguard the city's forest, the company even imported an ecologist from Yale to see whether one of its new lakes might somehow damage or affect adjacent woodland.

*Recreating vitality.*    By scaling the environment to the individual's needs and not leaving it simply to chance, Rouse hopes to reestablish vital urban interrelationships that most other cities smother or destroy. "Think of the constructive interactions of good housing, jobs, education, recreation, health, communication, and transportation," Rouse burbles infectiously. "Think how a good neighborhood environment might affect education, and how education, in turn, could affect the development of skills and how job training resources in a good neighborhood could influence new employment opportunities. Think how health and activity centers in such a neighborhood could help preventive medicine and health education work their way out to the people, how this might reduce critical illness, hospitalization, loss of time at work, and thus increase individual incomes, sense of well being, human effectiveness. And think how all of this together, in turn, might affect educability, employability, growth of the person, the family."

As it is now, says Rouse, the unplanned and uncoordinated "scatteration" of urban institutions is destroying the very society that they were created to serve—particularly in the ghetto. "Because a given neighborhood is ugly, dirty, dangerous," Rouse notes, "it has the most trouble getting good teachers. Poor education impedes growth in simple skills, limits employment opportunities. In turn, this leads to joblessness, idleness, delinquency, and crime. Business moves out or stays away because it is a bad neighborhood. Unemployment increases. Housing deteriorates. Slums are born—and grow." It is not enough, he adds, to tear down old buildings, put up new ones, and simply daub a fresh face on our cities. "The same forces that dragged them down in the first place would drag them down again. Good housing must replace bad housing. But good housing won't overcome the fear, despair, poor health, poor education, lack of skills, lack of hope. It won't create a neighborhood in which people feel safe and productive, a neighborhood that works for its people. That is the task we face today in the American city—to build neighborhoods that support and nourish the growth of the people who live there."

Some of Rouse's critics feel that he grossly oversimplifies today's social problems. "It's an extremely dubious proposition," ventures one New York social psychologist, "to claim that environment makes us what we are. History makes us what we are, and environment is only an extension of man—not the other way around." There can be no disputing the fact, however, that today's physical environment would profit by more planning and coordination, and that such planning—if not always solving our social problems—at least helps take our mind off them. Another equally indisputable fact is that Rouse and his company certainly have a broad and varied background on which to draw.

## Some Questions—
## and Some Discouraging Answers

Through its six offices around the country, Rouse Co. has financed over $1-billion in real estate development during the last 30 years, and owns or has under development for its own account more than $200-million in real estate projects in eight states and Canada. These projects include everything from apartment houses and office buildings to giant regional shopping centers such as Cherry Hill near Haddonfield, N. J. and North Star in San Antonio. As an evangelist of urban renewal, Rouse himself worked on President Eisenhower's Advisory Committee on Housing, and chaired the subcommittee that recommended the urban renewal program embraced in the Housing Act of 1954. He has also lectured on housing, design, and community development at Harvard, Johns Hopkins University, and the University of California; served as president of Urban America, Inc.; and is a member of the steering committee of the national Urban Coalition.

*A better way.*    Amid all these professional and extracurricular pursuits, Rouse says his company began asking itself some new questions eight or ten years ago. "Wasn't there a more rational way for a city to grow? Wasn't there a way to promote constructive interaction among houses, stores, offices, apartments, schools, churches, parks, and open spaces—if they could be planned for, provided for, and organized? Would it be possible to lay hold of a large enough tract of land to preserve the hills, stream valleys, and forest? Couldn't these hills and forests and stream valleys be used to give shape, separation, and identity to communities within the city?" And perhaps the biggest question of all: "Wouldn't it be very profitable to do this? Wouldn't it be even more profitable to develop a city this way rather than by the random manner in which they now grow?"

Rouse posed these questions—and received some discouraging answers. "We were told," he recalls, "that it was financially beyond us to undertake this, and that there was no developer in America who had the resources to go out and acquire the land to develop such a community." That answer was right—there wasn't. Rouse was also told that even if he had the money, he could not assemble that much land, and even if he lucked into an enormous piece of property, there would be holdouts who would prevent him from assembling the total package he needed. Then if he somehow got the money and the land, others told him he would almost certainly never get the zoning because people in the area would fight him. And most important of all, Rouse was advised that it was all utterly uneconomic—that the carrying charges alone on his investment in land acquisition and early planning would eat him alive.

*Self-perpetuating.* Rouse was undaunted. "In dealing with the American city," he says, "people are myopic about the roadblocks. They fail to identify a very special force that exists. And that force is simply that a big plan with real solutions to real problems will generate action and its own economics." Rouse then proceeded to generate some action on his own. The company built a hypothetical "model" for its new city, settled on a population of 110,000 as a target, and focused on the fast-growing corridor between Baltimore and Washington. Company planners determined how many jobs were needed to support such a population; how many homes, schools, stores, churches; how much recreation and open space. They came up with a figure of 14,000 acres and a land cost of $20-million.

With their preliminary estimates in hand, Rouse and his planners went to Frazar Wilde, board chairman of Connecticut General Life Insurance Co., which Rouse Co. had represented for 20 years as mortgage loan correspondent. "I told him," as Rouse recalls the conversation, "There is no developer in America who can finance this. The real resources available to the city building business are the great life insurance companies. Therefore, if this is to be done, you must provide the money for the land—not 80% or 90% of the money, but all of the money. Whatever we can put up is a pittance. We will do the planning and administer the program, but we need your financing." If the two companies bought the land at an average cost of $1,500 per acre—which they eventually did—the very worst that could happen was that Connecticut General would "get rich slowly. Who can get hurt owning 14,000 acres of land midway between Baltimore and Washington?" Wilde agreed, put up what eventually became $23.5-million, and Connecticut General acquired a half interest in the venture—representing the biggest single investment the company had ever made.

*Surprise announcement.*   That was early 1963. Right away, Rouse Co. quietly began buying up its land, and in nine months, assembled 149 separate farms and parcels totalling 14,000 acres. Armed with deeds and little more than an idea, Rouse and his planners walked into the office of the county commissioners of Maryland's Howard County and identified themselves for the first time as the owners of 10% of the county—a land area about the size of Manhattan. "This was quite an exciting experience," Rouse recalls with relish.

His Howard County neighbors were not nearly so excited. That was only a year after voters had tossed out a Democratic slate of county commissioners and elected their first Republicans in 40 years. The one single issue: a promise by the Republicans that they would preserve the county's rural character and low-density zoning. "I remember the first public meeting we had a few days after we announced the purchase," Rouse recalls. "One infuriated woman said, 'Do you mean to say you paid all that money for this land and you don't even have a plan?' I said, 'No, we have no plan. We are now going to make it.' They couldn't believe that this wasn't a sinister thing." Rouse's only assurance to her—and everyone else who initially opposed his new city—was that the company remained at their mercy. Unless it produced a plan which the public found better than the prospect of scattered, sprawling growth, they could reject the company's proposal and deny it zoning.

## Four Goals That Spelled Success

In putting together this plan itself, the company set out to satisfy four primary objectives.

*The first objective,* says Rouse, "was to build a real city, to provide what we would call a balanced city, a comprehensive city. We would be accounting as fully as we could for all the things that people do in a city of 110,000." The company analyzed the economic and employment base of such a city, determined the required number of primary jobs supplying goods and services (about 10,000) and the number of supporting jobs, such as school teachers, doctors, architects, and—yes—mortgage bankers (20,000). It added up the requirements of these people: 70 schools, 50 churches, a college, a hospital, department stores, shops, a concert hall, restaurants, hotels, and all the other myriad threads that go into the texture of a whole city.

*The second objective* was to "respect the land." The company identified every little side road, literally every grove of trees, every "significant vista," every historical building. Then it put these features on overlays so they began to exert an influence and discipline on how the community might emerge. "By staying away from the stream valleys and the forests," says Morton Hoppenfeld, Rouse's chief planner, "we were not simply being noble. We were being prudent. This meant that we were not bringing in the bulldozers into those areas where it would be the most expensive, the most extravagant, the most difficult, and the most brutal." The net result was that of the 14,000 acres of land, about 3,200 were set aside as permanent open space.

*The third objective* was to combine the people and the land, and create "the best possible environment for the growth of the people," says Rouse. "We really were not building apartments or houses or stores or roads or schools or churches or hospitals. What we were trying to do was provide for people." For this phase of the planning, the company brought together a group of 14 experts—not to blueprint a Utopian society, says Rouse, but to develop the same understanding about people as the company had tried to develop about the land.

The group met for two days every two weeks for six months to examine the processes and institutions by which people live. Rouse told the group that he did not want a report, or recommendations, or even agreement. He did not want to talk with an educator about education, a health man about health, nor a minister about religion. He wanted to explore all these disciplines acting, reacting, and interacting. "We want conversation in depth about man, his family, and his institutions," Rouse told them. "We want to allow your insights about people to influence the physical plan and guide us in stimulating within the community the kinds of programs in school, church, health, culture, recreation, and work that would support the growth of people."

With a shorter work week and increasing wages, for instance, what opportunities could be made available for better use of leisure time? How could music, art, theatre, adult education, physical recreation be provided in a way that guaranteed maximum participation and value? How could these and all the other institutions best interact? Could the church serve a need in counseling and become part of the health system? Could nurses and doctors, in turn, become part of the educational system? Should a library perhaps sell paperbacks? What size neighborhoods do people feel most comfortable in? The most creative? "Let's examine the optimums," Rouse suggested. "Don't worry about feasibility. It will compromise us soon enough."

Psychologist Donald N. Michael of Washington's Institute of Policy Studies felt that Rouse's city should have a land plan oriented toward people rather than buildings. "A good physical plan," he said, "can actually encourage social activities and individual growth." Stephen B. Withey of the University of Michigan's Institute of Social Research underlined the importance of a reliable communication network. He proposed an annual community report, closed-circuit television, a centralized information center, early creation of a city newspaper, and even a rumor-checking service. On the other hand, Washington economic consultant Robert Gladstone warned that the individual's privacy must be rigorously protected. "There's a lot of opposition in this country," he noted, "to the company town or the community that smacks of too much planning." Added another participant: "We don't want a place where someone rings your doorbell on Saturday morning and announces, 'Everybody out for shuffleboard.'"

Wayne Thompson, former city manager of Oakland, Calif. and a highly imaginative city planner, felt that people on a village level should try to form their own associations to handle garbage collection, street maintenance, and other housekeeping chores normally assumed by the government. "We have to turn loose the resources of the public sector for more urgent problems," he felt. At the "block" level, sociologist Herbert Gans of Columbia University stressed the importance of "block homogeneity." The block, he said, "is the major social arena, the major source of friends for most people. Putting well educated with poorly educated, working class with upper-middle class creates conflict. One cannot segregate by education or by child-rearing values. So price—which reflects income—is the developer's only form of leverage."

*The fourth objective* of the company's plan was to turn not just a profit—but an "outstanding profit," says Rouse. If Columbia was to influence the development of the American urban area and truly evolve as "the next America," as Hoppenfeld calls it, "then the company must prove that people really seek a better environment, and that business will want to locate there." To satisfy this fourth objective, Rouse Co. developed a highly sophisticated mathematical model, revised quarterly, that programs every stage of construction and every single expense. "This way," says Richard Anderson, general manager of Columbia, "everything we do is governed by logical decisions, rather than the guess-and-by-golly approach you get in most other projects like this."

## A City Begins to Take Shape

By the fall of 1964, the plan was completed and presented to the people and the county government. What they saw was a city that would stretch nine miles east and west and five miles north and south. At the center was to be a major downtown core that would include office buildings, department stores, hotels, restaurants, movies, concert hall, theatres, a main library, hospitals, and other major urban institutions. Beyond the core area, the city would break down into nine villages. Each village would have a population of 10,000 to 15,000 people, be separated from the other villages by stream valleys, parks, and bridle paths, and cluster around a village center complete with high school, middle school, branch library, churches, medical clinic, supermarkets, suburban shops, and so on. The villages, in turn, were to break down into four to six neighborhoods of 500 to 700 families each. At the center of each neighborhood would be a community center, child care center, playground, swimming pool, a small country store, and an elementary school. By scattering many small schools through the neighborhoods and villages and avoiding the usual large consolidated schools that normally develop, Rouse was able to eliminate the need for bussing. By

1980, at current bussing costs, that alone will mean a saving of more than $1-million a year.

When the neighboring Howard County residents had a chance to study Rouse's plan and saw what he was hoping to do, all the previous resistance to his ideas melted away. The result: not one person publicly opposed the zoning change. This was because, Rouse feels, "what the company offered was a sufficiently big image, and significantly big answer. It was so totally out of scale with all the pieces of urban sprawl that they had been fighting that they were willing to buy a complete city."

*Key endorsement.* Today, Columbia is a going concern. The original $23.5-million invested by Connecticut General has been followed by another $25-million from Chase Manhattan Bank and Teachers Insurance & Annuity Assn., as well as other investments by Morgan Guaranty Bank, Equitable Life Assurance Society, John Hancock Mutual Life Insurance Co., and several lenders in the Baltimore-Washington area. "This is a very important endorsement," says Bruce Hayden, Connecticut General's mortgage and real estate vice president.

The biggest endorsement, of course, has come from the people and companies moving to Columbia. So far, land has been sold to developers for 4,600 dwelling units, ranging from low-rent apartments to luxury lakefront aeries. The city's population is above 5,000, and expected to exceed 12,000 by mid-1970. Twenty-six industries and 83 businesses have rented space or acquired land. Among them is General Electric Co., which has started construction on a huge $250-million "Appliance Park East." The plant will employ 12,000 people by 1975, maintain a $100-million a year payroll, and constitute Maryland's third largest industry. Eastern Products Corp., Columbia's next largest industry, investigated 18 different locations before deciding on Columbia. "Our only complaint," says J. M. Scott, executive vice president of Eastern Products, "is a manpower shortage, which we hope is only temporary." Beyond that, says Scott, "the living is great. I have two kids—eight and nine years old—and there is something going on for them all the time: organized baseball, football, hikes. We have fishing only 200-ft. from our house." Merchants are just as enthusiastic. "The first year was rough," says William Jefferson, president of Columbia Bank & Trust Co. "You had several merchants here before there was any real purchasing public." But business is picking up now, and toward the end of 1969 was running 40% ahead of the year before. Today, Jefferson's three-year-old bank has 3,300 accounts and total assets of $7.5-million.

*Budding institutions.* As part of the city's pioneering spirit, Columbia's Catholics, Jews, and all 13 major Protestant denominations have pooled their resources and formed a joint ministry that shares both staff and church facilities—thus cutting costs and eliminating the usual struggle for individual church status. They have also formed the Columbia Interfaith Housing Corp., and in 1969 had 300 low-income dwelling units under construction. Equally innovative experiments are underway in the city's educational system. With a grant from the Ford Foundation, Columbia's elementary schools are experimenting with team teaching, electronic learning aids, and several curriculum changes.

Among the city's other budding educational and cultural institutions:

▪ Washington National Symphony, which makes its summer home at Columbia's Merriweather Post Pavilion of Music.

▪ Corcoran Gallery of Art, which conducts art courses in the city.

▪ Peabody Conservatory of Music, which runs dance classes.

▪ Antioch College, which began a Columbia program in the fall of 1969.

▪ Howard County Community College, now under construction on a site adjacent to downtown Columbia.

▪ Dag Hammarskjold College, a four-year, co-educational liberal arts college planning to open in 1970.

■ A permanent, professional repertory theatre group and a legitimate theatre, the Garland Dinner Theatre.

## Amid Kudos and Brickbats—a Triumph of Vision

Rouse has won many kudos for his new city. But he has also received his share of brickbats. "There is little at Columbia to strike joy in the hearts of design sophisticates," says Architectural Forum (which, oddly enough, is published by Urban America, of which Rouse is a past president). Much of the criticism is directed at the city's architecture. Detached houses follow the traditional lines of most subdivision houses, except that they are clustered in higher densities and surrounded by green areas. Apartments and town houses are mostly of an undistinguished contemporary design. Defenders point out that the town houses in Reston, Va., another new city, won plenty of architectural awards—but sold very slowly. Columbia's developers claim that they are tuned in to the marketplace, not the critics. Harvey G. Moger, one of four Connecticut General executives on Columbia's board of directors, admits that he is "disappointed in the appearance of houses at Columbia, but not in sales."

*Consolidation.* Rouse is the first to admit that there are no new approaches, as such, in Columbia—either in the architecture or the broader social planning. What is new is that Columbia pulls together many planning ideas tried in other cities, and often discontinued as failures. "These other efforts fail," says Rouse, "because they are isolated. Columbia succeeds because the efforts are interconnected, conceived, and presented in the context of a whole new urban pattern." Columbia also succeeds, Rouse adds, because it is the product of vision—and in the end, he feels that the triumph of this vision, as an example to others, may be the most important achievement to come out of Columbia. "Our real problem in the cities today," Rouse warns, "is not urban deterioration. It is a lack of vision, an inability to think on a grand scale and cope with the human and environmental problems behind urban deterioration. Image and vision are so important."

Rouse cites the case of some New York City officials who recently came to him for help on a small urban redevelopment project. "I was amazed," he recalls. "I looked at their map and there at the Southern end of Staten Island were 10,000 acres of undeveloped land. Here, they had a chance to build a whole new city, and had not recognized it. This was an unbelievable opportunity." The next week, Rouse was sitting next to New York's Mayor John Lindsay at a luncheon, and told him that he thought he could build this city without a nickel of subsidy. A few weeks later, Lindsay's government asked Rouse Co. to undertake a study and see if the idea was feasible. The study will be on the mayor's desk early in 1970.

"Some people in New York say things are not too bad," Rouse observes. "They point to all the new construction, the urban renewal, the air-conditioned subways. Sure, they say, we have some big and complicated problems. But New York is a big and complicated city. I say to that, you can't even walk the streets at night. You can almost fly to Washington faster than you get across town during the rush hour. The problem in New York and many other cities is that you have people who want to have vision, but can't because you can't have vision when you're in jail. And the average city today is a jail."

*Wrong measurement.*    There is a widespread misconception in America, Rouse feels, that our failure to deal adequately with these problems is a failure of the national government. Not so, he insists. "It is much more a failure of vision, of will. It is as if all the cities in the nation were engaged in a great battle that none of them expected to win. They lay out urban renewal programs, anti-poverty programs, highway and transportation programs, but fail to measure what it would take to fulfill all of these programs in their totality. It is as if we were building a variety of bridges across undetermined spans without measuring the cost of reaching the other side—and indeed without even expecting to arrive there."

Rouse insists that "it is easier to make our cities work than to deal with the problems deriving from their failure to work." Building a good city, he says, is an investment, while shoring up an old city amounts to throwing good money after bad. The tools and the knowledge are readily at hand to remake any American city into what we want it to be, he stresses. "The only missing force is a lack of conviction among the people and their leaders, a lack of determination to pick up the tools, put the knowledge to work, and make the city noble."

Rouse sees some hopeful signs on the urban horizon, however. In Hartford, Conn., 21 leading businessmen got together, raised a $2-million development fund, and hired Rouse Co. to come in and make a preliminary study of the city's total environment. Working closely with local people in and outside of government and business, Rouse Co. is now making a major exploration of Hartford's education, health, welfare, employment, housing, transportation, and other urban systems, and trying to discover what Hartford would be like if these systems could be coordinated and elevated to their highest potential. From there, Rouse Co. will propose how the city might reach that full potential, schedule the program for doing it, and lay out the arithmetic in capital costs and operating budgets both for the city and the larger region it occupies.

"For too long," Rouse observes, "people have been standing back and simply throwing darts at this big board we call the urban crisis. Our Hartford contract is encouraging in that it suggests that some communities are finally looking at these problems in their totality, and recognizing that the city—and its problems—are bigger than the sum of their parts." If this recognition is indeed sinking in, Rouse and his company are at least partly the reason.